20 EVENTS

Business Leaders

WHO BUILT FINANCIAL EMPIRES

JODINE MAYBERRY

BPMS
Media Center

RSVP

**RAINTREE
STECK-VAUGHN**
P U B L I S H E R S

The Steck-Vaughn Company

Austin, Texas

Consultant: Gary Gerstle, Department of History, The Catholic University of America, Washington, D.C.

Developed for Steck-Vaughn Company by
Visual Education Corporation, Princeton, New Jersey

Project Director: Jewel Moulthrop
Editor: Michael Gee
Copy Editor: Margaret P. Roeske
Editorial Assistants: Carol Ciaston, Stacy Tibbetts
Photo Research: Martin A. Levick
Production Supervisor: Maureen Ryan Pancza
Proofreading Management: William A. Murray
Word Processing: Cynthia C. Feldner
Interior Design: Maxson Crandall, Lee Grabarczyk
Cover Design: Maxson Crandall
Page Layout: Maxson Crandall, Lisa Evans-Skopas, Christine Osborne

Raintree Steck-Vaughn Publishers staff

Editor: Shirley Shalit
Project Manager: Joyce Spicer

Library of Congress Cataloging-in-Publication Data

Mayberry, Jodine.
    Business leaders who built financial empires / Jodine Mayberry.
        p.   cm. — (20 Events)
    Includes bibliographical references and index.
    ISBN 0-8114-4934-3
    1. Capitalists and financiers—United States—Biography—Juvenile literature.   2. Businessmen—United States—Biography—Juvenile literature. [1. Capitalists and financiers. 2. Businessmen.]
I. Title. II. Series.
HC102.5.A2M34 1995
338.092′273—dc20
[B]   94–13719
                                                                                                    CIP
                                                                                                    AC

Cover: In the mid-1970s, Stephen Jobs (inset) designed the first personal computer. By the mid-1980s, personal computers became a familiar sight in offices (background), schools, libraries, and homes throughout the world.

Credits and Acknowledgments

Cover photos: Visual Education Corporation (background), Reuters/Bettmann (inset)
Illustrations: Parrot Graphics, Precision Graphics

4: Levi Strauss & Co.; 5: Levi Strauss & Co.; 6: Library of Congress (left), Carnegie Library, Pittsburgh (right); 7: Carnegie Library; 8: The Bettmann Archive; 9: The Bettmann Archive (top), Catherine Ursillo/Photo Researchers (bottom); 10: Kellogg Company; 11: Kellogg Company; 12: Library of Congress (top), Sears (bottom); 13: Sears; 14: Library of Congress; 15: Culver Pictures, Inc. (top), John Blades/Hearst San Simeon State Historical Monument (bottom); 16: New York Public Library Picture Collection/© The Schomberg Center; 17: Brown Brothers; 18: Moulin Studios/Bank of America (top), Library of Congress (bottom); 19: Bank of America; 20: The Fuller Brush Company; 22: UPI/Bettmann; 23: UPI/Bettmann; 24: The Keystone Collection/Syndication International; 25: Times Newspaper, Ltd.; 26: UPI/Bettmann; 27: Globe Photos; 28: McDonald's Corporation; 29: McDonald's Corporation; 30: UPI/Bettmann; 31: Reuters/Bettmann; 32: Zavell's, Inc.; 33: Louie Psihoyos/Matrix; 34: Nike, Inc.; 35: Reuters/Bettmann; 36: D. Kirkland/Sygma (top), CNN (bottom); 37: CNN; 38: The Body Shop; 39: The Body Shop; 40: Ben and Jerry's; 41: Ben and Jerry's (top), Richard T. Nowitz (bottom); 42: Apple Computer, Inc.; 43: Apple Computer, Inc. (top), Reuters/Bettmann (bottom)

Contents

Levi Strauss

He made blue jeans for miners during the California gold rush and created a type of clothing that is still popular.

While developing durable work clothes, Levi Strauss created a style that is still fashionable.

The Gold Rush

In 1848, James Marshall discovered gold at Sutter's Mill, 100 miles northeast of San Francisco. Within a year, thousands of men rushed to the California goldfields. Before the arrival of the gold miners, San Francisco had been a sleepy settlement of only a few hundred people. By 1853, it had been transformed into a large, bustling city. Its population had grown to 70,000. The city had many stores, restaurants, hotels, and banks. Miners shopped in San Francisco for the tools, clothing, and supplies they needed to work on their gold claims.

One item miners needed, but could not find, was pants durable enough to withstand the rigors of digging and panning for gold. A German Jewish immigrant named Levi Strauss solved that problem for them. Strauss was born in Bavaria in 1829 and came to the United States in 1847. He joined two older brothers who had emigrated earlier and settled in New York City. The brothers had established themselves in the dry goods business. Dry goods are fabrics, clothing, and sewing items.

The Life of a Peddler Like many 19th-century Jewish immigrants, Levi Strauss became a peddler. He tramped from door to door carrying his wares in a heavy pack on his back. About the same time that gold was discovered in California, Levi's sister Fanny married a man named David Stern. The young couple moved to San Francisco to open a dry goods store. Stern invited Strauss to join them in San Francisco.

The Birth of the Blue Jeans

Strauss, then 24, set out on the five-month ocean voyage (this was before the first transcontinental railroad). He brought with him a large quantity of merchandise, nearly all of which he sold to other passengers before the ship docked in San Francisco. The only item he had left was a roll of brown canvas intended for tents and wagon covers. Legend has it that when Strauss offered his canvas cloth for sale, a miner told him, "Should'a brought pants. Pants don't wear a hoot in the diggin's."

Strauss took the canvas to a tailor and had him turn the material into several pairs of work pants. Strauss's work pants sold quickly and became very popular. He continued to make the pants out of canvas for a while. Then one day he purchased a shipment of work clothes made from *serge de Nîmes,* a strong, durable fabric made in Nîmes, France. (Today we know the fabric as denim.) After that, Strauss found a mill in New Hampshire that could make denim for him, and he bought the fabric there.

Copper Rivets By 1861, Levi Strauss & Co. was a large wholesale clothing business. Strauss continued to manufacture his denim pants, parceling out the work to tailors throughout the area. Then, in 1872, a Nevada tailor named Jacob Davis wrote to Strauss with an idea. Davis suggested reinforcing the corners of the pockets with copper rivets. This would enable them to hold heavy gold nuggets without tearing. Davis

The "501" jeans have changed little over the past century from those worn by these miners in Placer County, California, in 1882.

easier fittin'...workin' or sittin'...

LEVI'S*
AMERICA'S FINEST
OVERALL
SINCE 1850

PATRONIZE YOUR HOMETOWN MERCHANT...HE'S YOUR NEIGHBOR!
* THE NAME LEVI'S IS REGISTERED IN THE U.S. PATENT OFFICE AND DENOTES OVERALLS AND OTHER GARMENTS MADE ONLY BY LEVI STRAUSS & CO.

Eventually, the company began manufacturing jeans for women and children, as this advertisement shows.

needed Strauss's help in obtaining a patent on the riveted pockets. The two men went into business together to produce the pants. They built a factory on Fremont Street in San Francisco and hired 60 women to make the pants on modern sewing machines.

Levi's Jeans Levi Strauss called his pants "waist high overalls." Many people who purchased Strauss's pants simply called them "Levi's" after the name of the company that made them. Others called them "jeans," a word derived from cheap cotton sailors' trousers manufactured in Genoa, Italy. In 1886, the Levi Strauss company added a leather patch to a back pocket of its jeans with an image of two horses attempting to pull apart a pair of Levi's jeans. (In 1913, Strauss guaranteed that the company would replace any pair of its pants free if they ripped.)

Today, the company offers pants, skirts, jackets, and shirts in many different styles and colors.

More Popular Than Ever

The Levi Strauss company flourished. Strauss himself became a prominent member of both the business community and the Jewish community in San Francisco. His brother-in-law and business partner, David Stern, died in 1874. Strauss, who had never married or had children, turned the company's management over to his nephews, Stern's sons. He wished to concentrate on other business and charitable activities. He donated some of his money to local charities, such as the Hebrew Board of Relief, the Eureka Benevolent Society, and the Pacific Hebrew Orphan Asylum. He also funded 28 scholarships at the University of California.

After Levi When Levi Strauss died in 1902, his four nephews inherited the company. Their descendants still own it. At the time of his death, Levi Strauss's jeans were already being worn throughout the western United States, not only by miners, but also by ranchers, farmers, cowboys, and factory workers. By the 1930s, their popularity was spreading east. Easterners taking vacations on Western "dude" ranches (tourist ranches) took jeans back home with them. During World War II, jeans became part of the uniform of workers who built planes and ships for the war effort.

In the 1950s, popular movies such as *Rebel Without a Cause* and *The Wild Ones* featured jeans-clad young stars, making the pants immensely popular with teenagers. They are still the single most popular item of clothing in America today. The Levi Strauss company now produces many kinds of clothing at dozens of factories around the world. In 1976, the Smithsonian Institution added a pair of Levi's jeans to its historical clothing collection. Levi Strauss, the man, is gone and largely forgotten, but his first name has become part of the world's vocabulary.

Andrew Carnegie

After amassing one of America's greatest fortunes, this steel manufacturer spent the rest of his life giving it away.

Accustomed to hard work from an early age, Andrew Carnegie built one of the largest steelmaking companies in the world.

In 1897, *Scientific American* featured the Carnegie steel mill in Homestead, Pennsylvania, in its magazine. Several years earlier, the Homestead plant had been the site of one of the most disastrous workers' strikes in American labor history. The strike ended with several people dead and the collapse of the union.

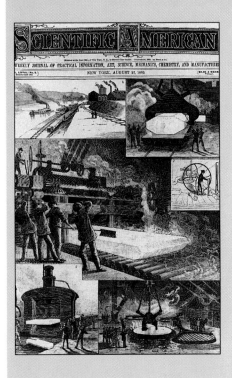

The Industrial Revolution

The invention of the steam engine at the end of the 18th century marked the beginning of the Industrial Revolution. The steam engine enabled people to mass-produce goods by machine instead of making them slowly and laboriously by hand. Before the Industrial Revolution, most craftspeople worked in their own homes making items to sell. In the years that followed, people went to work in factories to run the machines that made the goods.

William Carnegie—the father of Andrew Carnegie—was one of the craftspeople affected by the Industrial Revolution. He was a weaver who worked at home at a hand loom in the Scottish village of Dunfermline. He made fine linen cloth out of flax. By the middle of the 19th century, however, most cloth was already being woven by machine. Weavers like Will Carnegie could no longer make a living. In 1848, Carnegie sold his loom and took his wife, Margaret, and his two young sons, Andrew and Tom, to America. Little did they know that Andrew would himself become one of the greatest captains of the industrial age.

From Bobbin Boy to Tycoon

The Carnegie family settled in Allegheny City, Pennsylvania, a small town that later became part of Pittsburgh. Will Carnegie tried weaving again but could not make a go of it. Will's wife assembled shoes. Twelve-year-old Andrew went to work in a cotton factory. He worked 12 hours a day tending the thread bobbins (spools) for $1.20 a week.

Two years later, Andrew took a better-paying job as a messenger boy for a Pittsburgh telegraph office. He soon became a telegraph operator. When a Pittsburgh businessman established a lending library for workers, Carnegie borrowed many books. He completed his education by reading a wide variety of books, especially ones on technology.

Hired by the Railroad Through his telegraph work, Carnegie met Thomas Scott, a superintendent of the Pennsylvania Railroad. Scott hired him to operate the railroad's telegraph office for $35 a month. Scott was very impressed with the energetic and resourceful young man and came to rely on him more and more. Once, when Scott was away, Carnegie was faced with a problem—a boxcar that was blocking the tracks. He solved the problem by burning down the car. When Scott became president of the railroad in 1859, he promoted Carnegie to manager of the Pittsburgh division. During the Civil War, Carnegie accompanied Scott to Washington, where they organized transportation and telegraph communications for the Union Army.

The Investor As Carnegie's position and finances improved, he began investing in other companies, including a sleeping car company and an oil refinery. He became a partner in the Keystone Bridge Company, which specialized in building iron bridges. By the age of 33, he was making more than $50,000 a year from his investments, a very large sum for that time. Carnegie resigned from the Pennsylvania Railroad in 1865 to concentrate on the rapidly growing steel industry.

The Steel Age Dawns Steel is manufactured from iron ore; but it is much stronger and more durable than iron. In Carnegie's time, however, steel was very expensive to manufacture. On a trip to England in the 1870s, Carnegie learned about Henry Bessemer's new process for making steel stronger and making it more cheaply. In 1873, Carnegie formed a new company to build a Bessemer steel plant in Braddock, a town outside Pittsburgh.

Carnegie's company was soon making about one-seventh of all the steel produced in the United States. Gradually, he strengthened his hold on the steelmaking industry. He bought coalfields, iron ore mines, and steamships, all of which were needed to manufacture and transport his products.

As time passed, Carnegie became an immensely wealthy man. Little by little he turned the operation of his businesses over to others. He divided his time between homes in Scotland and New York City. In 1901, Carnegie sold his steel company to banker J. P. Morgan for $400 million. Morgan combined Carnegie Steel with other steelworks to form the giant United States Steel Corporation.

The Gospel of Wealth

Carnegie spent the rest of his life giving away his vast fortune. He believed that it was disgraceful to die excessively rich. His first gift was a $4 million relief and pension fund for his workers. He also provided private pensions for more than 400 friends and relatives. Remembering the lending library where he had completed his own education, Carnegie spent more than 20 years endowing 2,800 libraries throughout the United States, Canada, and Great Britain. Many of the libraries were named for him.

His other gifts were equally far-reaching. Andrew Carnegie

- established a $4 million trust fund for his birthplace, Dunfermline.
- founded the Carnegie Institute of Technology in Pittsburgh.
- established the Carnegie Institution for scientific research in Washington, D.C.
- built the Mount Wilson Observatory in California.
- built Carnegie Hall in New York City.

Deeply interested in promoting world peace, he paid for the construction of the World Court building at The Hague in the Netherlands and established the Carnegie Endowment for International Peace. By the time Carnegie died in 1919, he had succeeded in giving away more than $330 million.

"Surplus wealth is a sacred trust which its possessor is bound to administer in his lifetime for the good of the community."

Andrew Carnegie, 1889

Andrew Carnegie believed that wealth should be used to benefit the community. He was especially generous in his gifts to libraries.

John D. Rockefeller

His oil monopoly made
him the richest man
in the world and
a great philanthropist.

The New Industrial Giant

By the late 1800s, railroads had spread across the United States. American cities were growing fast and new kinds of industries were developing. Entrepreneurs (people who own businesses), emerging from the Civil War with great fortunes, were increasing their wealth by investing in mining, shipping, and manufacturing.

A New Source of Light In 1859, E. L. Drake drilled the world's first oil well in Titusville, Pennsylvania. This was long before the internal combustion engine and automobiles were invented. But scientists had already found one important use for crude oil. It was refined into kerosene to light lamps. Before the development of kerosene, people had to rely on candles, which gave off a poor light, or whale oil lamps, which were smoky and smelly. Kerosene improved on these because it burned cleanly, brightly, and slowly.

In the oil boom that followed, John D. Rockefeller wisely invested his money and talents in the new enterprise of oil refining. He helped develop it into the major industry it is today.

A Boy in the City John D. Rockefeller was born in Tioga County, New York, in 1839. He was a solemn, reserved, and ambitious boy who first learned about business from his flamboyant father, William Rockefeller. Known as "Big Bill," the elder Rockefeller made his living buying and selling land and traveling around the countryside selling fake medicines. "I cheat my boys every chance I get," his father once said. "I want to make them sharp." However, John D. also acquired a sense of propriety and righteousness from his stern, religious mother, Eliza.

In 1853, when John D. Rockefeller turned 14, his father took him to the bustling port city of Cleveland, Ohio. There Big Bill enrolled his son in high school, found a room in a boardinghouse for him, and left him on his own. Never an outgoing person, John D. made few friends in school. He did meet his future wife, Laura Celestia Spelman, there, however. He also joined a nearby Baptist church, where he became a leading member of the congregation.

By gaining control over related oil industry businesses, Rockefeller built one of the first U.S. monopolies.

The Rise of Rockefeller

Standard Oil After his graduation from high school in 1855, Rockefeller took a job in a Cleveland wholesale firm that sold grain and other food products. He earned $4 a week. By the age of 20, he had learned so much about the business that he was able to start his own wholesaling firm with a partner named Maurice Clark. In 1863, Rockefeller, Clark, and a few others invested $4,000 in an oil refining company. Two years later, Rockefeller bought out his partners' shares in the refinery. Teamed with an oil-refining expert named Samuel Andrews, he focused his energy on the kerosene business.

In his careful way, Rockefeller set out to study the new industry he had entered. He soon realized that in order to maximize his profits, he needed to gain control of as many aspects of the industry as he could from bottom to top—drilling, refining, shipping, and selling. In 1870, Rockefeller incorporated his oil company under the name of the Standard Oil Company of Ohio. Gradually, he bought out many competitors and drove others to bankruptcy. By 1880, Standard Oil controlled nearly all the oil business in the United States.

The Standard Oil Trust Maintaining control over such a vast corporation was an unprecedented task. Rockefeller faced legal hurdles in laws that were meant to discourage monopolies as well as practical challenges in managing Standard Oil's nationwide holdings. In response, a company lawyer devised a new kind of organization for industry called a "trust." In a trust, a board of trustees or directors maintains centralized control over a group of separate companies. Through the Standard Oil

Rockefeller came under severe criticism for his business practices. The artist of this 1905 cartoon expresses the view that Rockefeller was ruthless in destroying the competition.

The Works Continue

Rockefeller's oil business made him so wealthy that the phrase "rich as Rockefeller" became a common term for describing anyone with great wealth. He lived to the age of 97. In his later years, he was a familiar sight on the streets of New York City, giving shiny, new dimes to people he encountered. By the time Rockefeller died in 1937, he had given more than $500 million to charitable causes. The four foundations he established were merged into the Rockefeller Foundation. To this day, it is still the largest private charitable foundation in the world.

Rockefeller's son, John D. Rockefeller Jr., continued his father's work until his own death in 1960. He provided the money to restore Colonial Williamsburg in Virginia and to build Rockefeller Center in New York City. Pieces of the Standard Oil Company still operating today include the major oil companies Amoco, Atlantic Richfield, BP America (formerly Sohio), Chevron, Exxon, and Mobil.

Millions of visitors enjoy the ice-skating rink and other attractions of Rockefeller Center.

Trust, Rockefeller retained a monopoly over the kerosene industry while steering around the laws at that time.

However, the public became alarmed at the dominance of Standard Oil. Rockefeller was harshly criticized in the press for business practices that eliminated competition. Many people resented him personally for his wealth and power.

A Passion for Good Works Based on stronger antitrust laws, the U.S. Supreme Court broke up Standard Oil in 1911 and divided it into several independent companies. By then, Rockefeller had long since ceased to be active in the business. He had always given a portion of his fortune to charity each year. Now he turned his attention to distributing his great wealth in a more systematic way. In 1890, he founded the University of Chicago with an initial grant of $600,000, which at that time was a huge sum of money. Then he established four separate foundations—one to fund medical research, one to support health and education programs in the rural South, and one for social science research. The fourth, the Rockefeller Foundation, was "to promote the well-being of mankind throughout the world."

W. K. Kellogg

In helping his brother invent a breakfast cereal, he built one of the world's largest breakfast food companies.

Will Kellogg began his successful career as the business manager at his brother's medical treatment and rehabilitation center.

A Tale of Two Kelloggs

Battle Creek Will Keith Kellogg's parents, John and Ann Kellogg, were members of the Seventh-day Adventists, a Christian group that stresses healthful living and vegetarianism. John Kellogg moved his family to Battle Creek, Michigan, in the 1850s. At that time the town was a center of Adventism. Will Kellogg was born in Battle Creek in 1860.

One of Will's older brothers, John Harvey Kellogg, became a physician and rose to prominence as the head of the Adventists' Western Health Reform Institute in Battle Creek. Will, however, dropped out of school at age 14. He worked as a broom salesman, then enrolled in business school. With his energy and ability, he completed a year of course work in four months.

The San In 1880, Will Kellogg went to work for his brother at the institute. He ran its business operations. By then, the institute's name had been changed to the Battle Creek Sanitarium. The "San," as it was commonly called, was a place for medical treatment and rehabilitation. Under Dr. John Kellogg, it had become world famous for its program of healthful diet and exercise. It was there that Will Kellogg would launch his own career as the world's foremost maker of breakfast cereals.

The Kelloggs' Breakfast

Accidental Flakes Vegetarian and natural foods were an important part of the sanitarium's program. Dr. Kellogg started a food company to supply the sanitarium. Will managed this business, which also included a laboratory where new foods were developed. One of the experiments involved making a product out of wheat that patients could digest more easily than bread. The experiments had failed several times. But one day, a batch of wheat that had accidentally stood in water all night was run through rollers, and wheat flakes came out. The brothers realized that this was the product they had been looking for. The cereal, which they called Granose, became so popular that patients continued ordering it after they left the sanitarium.

Kellogg's Corn Flakes Although the Kelloggs tried to keep their process for making cereal flakes secret, it eventually leaked out, and dozens of other cereal companies started up in Battle Creek. Meanwhile, the brothers continued to experiment. In 1898, they developed a new version of the flakes made out of corn. Will wanted to sell the new cereal to the general public, but John

Research and production take place at Kellogg's Battle Creek Production Facility and Science and Technology Complex, shown here.

10

was reluctant. Although Will Kellogg worked for his brother for nearly 20 years, the two men argued frequently, and Will often resented his domineering brother. In 1901, Will quit his job at the sanitarium but continued to run the food company for several years.

A Corn Flake Company Will Kellogg finally struck out on his own in 1906. With the backing of an investor, he built a factory and began making Kellogg's Corn Flakes. He called his company the Battle Creek Toasted Corn Flake Company.

Faced with many competitors, Kellogg relied on creative promotional techniques to push his product ahead. Early on, he took samples of his cereal door-to-door to tell people that it was the original and other brands were merely imitations. Each box of his cereal carried the slogan, "None genuine without this signature—W. K. Kellogg." The word Kellogg's in Will's handwriting remains the company trademark to this day. Kellogg also advertised heavily, spending into the millions. In 1912, he erected the world's largest advertising sign in Times Square, a busy intersection in New York City.

The Brothers Fall Out In 1909, Dr. John Kellogg, who by then was selling his own cereals, sued Will over the use of the Kellogg name. The bitter lawsuit lasted until 1921, when Will Kellogg won the exclusive right to use the family name. His company continued to grow rapidly. In the 1920s, it began making other cereals besides Corn Flakes. By 1930, it was a truly international business, with manufacturing plants in Canada, Australia, and England. Today, the Kellogg Company has plants in 18 countries and distributes products to more than 150 countries.

The Cereal King

Much to his surprise, Will Kellogg became a millionaire and then a multimillionaire. When the company treasurer informed Kellogg that he was a millionaire, he gasped and said, "I am no such thing!"

A progressive factory owner, Kellogg provided a nursery for the children of his female workers and a clinic to care for their medical and dental needs. During the Great Depression of the 1930s, he added more shifts so that he could employ more people.

As successful as he was in business, W. K. Kellogg was much less successful in his personal life. He was very stern and spent little time with his wife and children. His feud with his brother lasted until John Kellogg's death in 1943.

Helping Children Although distant with his own children, Kellogg dedicated his huge fortune to helping other children. In 1930, he created the W. K. Kellogg Child Welfare Foundation to promote the health, happiness, and well-being of children. The foundation funded the Michigan Community Health Project in the 1930s to bring health care to the state's rural children. Today, the Kellogg Foundation has broadened its mission to "help people help themselves." It has donated more than $1.8 billion for various educational, agricultural, health, and volunteer projects as well as projects that help children around the world.

A Long Life Blinded by disease in his later years, Kellogg was often seen walking near his company headquarters in Battle Creek with his guide dog. He donated generously to the Battle Creek community, creating hospitals, schools, parks, and a community college. He gave his three estates in Florida, Michigan, and California to public institutions. When Kellogg died in 1951 at the age of 91, he had succeeded in making Battle Creek the "cereal capital of the world."

In 1994, the company celebrated Bonnie Blair's Olympic victory in speed skating by putting her picture on the Corn Flakes box. It is shown here with a box from the early 1900s.

BPMS
Media Center

Richard Sears

Sears's mail order catalogs brought reasonably priced, mass-produced goods to rural America.

Richard Sears, who grew up in a rural area, helped farm families buy the products that were readily available to urban dwellers.

A Store in a Book

The Sears Catalog Richard Sears kept ordering more watches and selling them in the same way. Within six months, he had earned $5,000, enough to quit his railroad job and establish the R. W. Sears Watch Company in Minneapolis. He advertised his business in the local newspapers—which was not commonly done at the time—and soon discovered that he had a gift for writing persuasive copy. His business grew quickly. He decided to relocate to a larger city, Chicago, and to distribute a catalog of his goods.

The Wish Book Sears's first catalog was only a few pages and featured mostly watches. His copywriting genius was perfectly suited to winning the trust of farmers. He offered lower prices than his competitors, and he guaranteed to replace defective products or refund the buyers' money. By 1892, the Sears catalog had grown to more than 100 pages and offered such items as clothing, musical instruments, and farm machinery.

Nation of Farmers

The United States in the 1800s was largely a nation of farmers. In the 1880s, 70 percent of Americans lived in the country, and agriculture was a major occupation. Millions of small family farms dotted the Midwest, isolated by distance from big cities such as St. Louis, Milwaukee, and Chicago. New inventions were making farm life easier, and the incomes of farmers were rising. While small town general stores provided the necessities, farm families wanted to purchase the consumer goods and fashions available in the big cities. The man who gave rural America the opportunity to buy "big city" goods was Richard Sears.

Selling Pocket Watches Richard Sears was born in 1863 and grew up in rural Minnesota. As a young man, he went to work in St. Paul as an agent for the Minneapolis and St. Louis Railroad. One day, a local jeweler rejected a shipment of gold-plated pocket watches from Chicago. Sears, then 23, agreed to purchase

the watches for $12 each. He then sold the watches to other railroad agents along the railway line for $14 each. They, in turn, sold the watches to local farmers for higher prices and pocketed the profit. That shipment of watches was the beginning of what would one day become the largest retail business in the world.

When the first retail store opened in Chicago in 1925, these shoppers were among the first to enjoy across-the-counter shopping at Sears.

Receiving the catalog, which came to be called the "wish book," was a big event in the lives of most rural people. Browsing in its pages, they could dream about owning the latest gadgets or wearing the latest fashions. It helped them learn about the wider world and enabled them to shop even though they were hundreds of miles from a department store.

Sears, Roebuck and Co. In 1887, a year after Sears started his watch company, he had advertised for a watchmaker to assemble and repair watches. When watchmaker Alvah C. Roebuck answered the ad, Sears promptly hired him and later took him on as a partner. The company adopted the name Sears, Roebuck and Co. in 1893. But it was not a happy partnership. After two years, Roebuck sold his half of the business to Sears.

Richard Sears was primarily a salesman and a promoter. "He could probably sell a breath of air," a business associate once said of him. However, he was not as good at operating a business. He often received more orders than he could fill and bought more goods than he could sell. He needed someone who could run the company in a more businesslike way. That person was Julius Rosenwald, a Chicago clothing maker. In 1895, Rosenwald became Sears's business partner.

By the turn of the century, Sears was sending out more than 318,000 catalogs each year. Orders flooded in faster than they could be filled. Rosenwald convinced Sears to build a huge new warehouse and distribution plant to process the orders. When the new plant opened in 1906, it enabled the company to fill 100,000 orders a day.

A cover from one of the last Sears catalogs is shown here. The catalog was often referred to as the "wish book."

Beginnings and Endings

Sears Bows Out Sears was totally devoted to his company, putting in long hours every day. But by 1908, both he and his wife were in poor health. Also, he began to have serious differences with Rosenwald over the running of the company. That year, Sears sold his shares for $10 million and resigned as president, leaving Rosenwald in charge. Although Sears held the title of chairman of the board for four more years, he never attended a board meeting. Sears died at the age of 50 in 1914.

Although Richard Sears left the company in its early years, he laid the foundation for much of its future growth. Sears was not afraid to try out new ideas, such as sending free catalogs and offering installment credit to his customers. In the years after Sears's departure, the Sears company continued his tradition of experimenting with new marketing ideas.

Solid as Sears Sears, Roebuck and Co. expanded steadily throughout much of the 20th century, opening thousands of retail stores and catalog stores in large cities and small towns across America. In the 1940s and 1950s, with the growth of suburbs and automobile use, the company built many retail stores in suburban shopping centers and malls. In 1974, the Sears company constructed the world's tallest building—the Sears Tower in Chicago—for its corporate headquarters.

The Sears company today does business in insurance as well as retail sales. In 1993, more than a hundred years after Richard Sears mailed his first catalog to farmers, Sears, Roebuck and Co. discontinued its catalog business. Americans' needs had changed over that time, and thanks in part to the legacy of Richard Sears, American retailers had changed with them.

William Randolph Hearst

His formula for successful newspapers had a great impact on news reporting and enabled him to build a media empire.

The Penny Press

During the 19th century, many technological developments made it possible for newspapers to reach a mass audience. New Linotype machines speeded up typesetting, and faster presses could print thousands of copies of each edition. Other innovations helped newspapers become more current and appealing. New machines allowed papers to print photographs and cartoons for the first time. New communications devices, such as the telephone and the telegraph, enabled reporters to transmit news almost instantaneously from one place to another. William Randolph Hearst used this new technology to deliver lively, entertaining newspapers to America's urban population at pennies a copy.

William Randolph Hearst was born in 1863 in San Francisco, California. He was the only child of George Hearst, a wealthy miner and politician, and his wife, Phoebe. Hearst attended Harvard University from 1882 until he was expelled for playing a practical joke. While Hearst was at Harvard, however, he became interested in newspapers.

William Randolph Hearst was only 24 years old when his father gave him control of the *San Francisco Examiner.*

A Media Empire

George Hearst had purchased the *San Francisco Examiner* in 1880. When he was elected to Congress in 1887, he turned the newspaper over to his son. William Randolph Hearst set about reorganizing it. He purchased new equipment and hired the most talented journalists and writers available. Following the model of publisher Joseph Pulitzer's successful *New York World,* the revamped *Examiner* contained accounts of scandals, murders, and political corruption. It was written in a simple and entertaining style designed to appeal to less sophisticated readers.

Conquering New York Soaring circulation figures (the average number of copies sold each day) proved that Hearst's ideas sold newspapers. Encouraged by his success, he purchased the *New York Journal.* With this purchase, and with $5 million supplied by his mother, he began to compete head-to-head with Pulitzer's *New York World.* One of Hearst's most successful strategies was to hire away several of the *World*'s best writers, editors, and managers. He even lured R. F. Outcault, the creator of the first newspaper comic strip, "The Yellow Kid."

Yellow Journalism By the 1890s, Hearst and Pulitzer were engaged in a lively competition for readers. Both aimed in particular at New York's newly arrived European immigrants, who did not read English well. The competition led to many theatrical stunts, crusades, and exposés (stories that uncovered scandal). One observer coined the phrase "yellow journalism" to describe the activities of the Hearst and Pulitzer newspapers. The term referred to journalism that was more concerned with sensationalism

NAVAL OFFICERS THINK THE MAINE WAS DESTROYED BY A SPANISH MINE.

Bold, sensational headlines, such as these during the Spanish-American War, were a trademark of the Hearst newspapers.

and entertainment than with providing objective, factual reporting.

Yellow journalism reached its peak in 1898. Hearst and other newspaper publishers shamelessly promoted U.S. intervention in the Cuban revolt against Spain. Hearst had sent the well-known American artist Frederick Remington to Cuba to draw pictures of the revolt. When Remington found little to draw there, Hearst supposedly telegraphed his orders: "You supply the pictures and I'll furnish the war." Whether or not the story is true, Hearst's newspapers blamed Spain for the mysterious explosion of the U.S. battleship *Maine* in Havana Harbor. (The explosion was later traced to an engine malfunction.) The newspaper accounts, however, helped whip public opinion into a frenzy of war fever.

A Growing Empire Following the war, Hearst kept adding to his chain of newspapers—in cities such as Boston, Los Angeles, Atlanta, and San Francisco. He also acquired several magazines—including *Cosmopolitan, Good Housekeeping,* and *Harper's Bazaar*—and started some new ones.

Building Castles

Political Failure While building his newspaper empire, Hearst decided to follow his father into politics. In 1902, he was elected to Congress from New York City. While serving in Congress, he tried to gain the Democratic nomination for President but lost. He also lost bids to become mayor of New York City in 1905 and governor of New York State in 1906.

Following his defeat in the governor's race, Hearst withdrew from politics. But he continued to exert political influence behind the scenes and through his newspapers. Always a political independent, Hearst became increasingly conservative as his business empire grew. His papers endorsed the liberal candidate for President, Franklin Roosevelt, in 1932. But Hearst later opposed him.

Life in Hollywood By 1920, Hearst owned more than 24 newspapers and magazines. He had also established a company to produce newsreels for movie theaters. He moved to Hollywood in 1924. During the "Roaring Twenties," when business was booming, Hearst spent much of his large

fortune building a castle, San Simeon, in California. Then he bought millions of dollars' worth of art and antiques to fill it. His excessive spending nearly exhausted his wealth during the Great Depression. He was forced to give up financial control of his properties. By the end of World War II in 1945, however, Hearst had reclaimed his media empire and rebuilt his personal fortune.

After Hearst Hearst died in 1951, at the age of 83, leaving $59.5 million to his heirs. His son, William Randolph Hearst Jr., took over management of the Hearst newspapers, which today form a major chain of more than 20 papers. The elder Hearst's flamboyant style of journalism is no longer popular. He is remembered today largely as a promoter and a showman rather than as a journalist.

The estate, which Hearst called "The Enchanted Hill," is now a California historical monument.

Madame C. J. Walker

This poor, uneducated washerwoman became the first African American woman millionaire.

A Sharecropper's Daughter

Sarah Breedlove was born in Delta, Louisiana, in 1867. She was the daughter of former slaves who had become sharecroppers after the Civil War. Sharecroppers are farmers who lease their land from the landowner in exchange for a portion of their harvest. Sarah's parents died when she was seven years old. She married a laborer at 14 and had a daughter, Lelia, three years later. When her husband was killed in an accident, she moved to St. Louis, Missouri. For the next 18 years, she took in laundry for $1.50 a day while she raised her daughter and put her through college.

Sarah Breedlove suffered from thinning hair, a condition that led her to try various hair-care products. Not satisfied, she began experimenting with her own compounds. She eventually hit on a set of preparations that gave her good results. Breedlove felt that other black women would like them as well. Starting with a few dollars' worth of chemicals, she mixed batches of the products in her washtub and began to sell them door-to-door to friends and neighbors.

The Walker System

In 1905, Sarah Breedlove moved to Denver, Colorado. There she met and married a Denver newspaperman named Charles J. Walker. Walker contributed his experience in advertising and promotion to his wife's small business. He gave her products a name—the "Walker System." The marriage did not last, primarily because Walker wanted his wife to remain in Denver and operate her business locally. She, on the other hand, had bigger plans. Although the marriage ended, Sarah Breedlove always called herself Madame C. J. Walker.

A New Look The Walker System consisted of a shampoo that soothed the scalp and a pomade, or ointment, that conditioned the hair. She called the pomade "Walker's Hair Grower" because it was supposed to stimulate hair growth. When used with a heated comb, the pomade made the curly hair of black women smooth and straight.

Straight hairstyles became popular with African American women of the time, many of whom aspired to the white image of beauty that was promoted in newspapers and magazines. The popular black entertainer Josephine Baker, whose own hair was straightened, enthusiastically endorsed Madame Walker's products. Some African Americans, however, criticized Walker for promoting the desire of black women to "look white." But Walker believed that her products gave women flexibility in their hairstyles and freedom to choose how they looked.

A Family Concern Madame Walker began traveling around the country demonstrating and selling her products to African American women at

Madame Walker, at the wheel of the car, used her great wealth to help other African American women become educated and independent.

churches, clubs, and private homes. She put her daughter Lelia in charge of overseeing the business and manufacturing. The enterprise grew rapidly. In 1908, Walker expanded to the East. She established a business office in Pittsburgh, Pennsylvania. Two years later, she built a large manufacturing plant in Indianapolis. The factory eventually employed more than 3,000 people.

Walker Agents To market her products, Madame Walker recruited and trained a team of door-to-door sellers. She called them "Walker agents." The agents, mostly African American women, signed a contract agreeing to follow her hygienic system and use her products. The Walker agents—dressed in crisp white blouses and long black skirts—became a familiar sight in African American communities throughout the United States. Madame Walker's sales force was knocking on doors long before other cosmetic companies began sending their saleswomen into American homes.

Madame Walker organized 200 local and state clubs of Walker agents. The purposes of these organizations were to support the agents and to promote the Walker products. The clubs held regular conventions at which they shared beauty techniques and business experiences. Walker advertised her products in African American newspapers and magazines. She also promoted her products through several beauty schools that she established. These schools trained black women to be hairdressers. Walker insisted on high standards of cleanliness in her beauty schools. Many states later adopted these standards into their own regulations governing the operation of beauty shops and schools.

Taking the first two letters of her daughter's names (Lelia Walker Robinson), Madame Walker called her estate *Villa Lewaro*. It is in Irvington, New York.

A Millionairess

Self-Made Woman Madame C. J. Walker's hair-care business made her America's first black female millionaire. Indeed, she was the first American woman to become a millionaire through her own business. In 1913, Walker and her daughter (who had changed her first name to A'Lelia) built a townhouse in Harlem, in New York City. During this time, Harlem was becoming a mainly African American community, as blacks from other parts of the city and from the rural South migrated there. Walker also built a 34-room mansion along the Hudson River in Irvington, New York. It was designed by African American architect Vertner Tandy.

Self-conscious about her lack of education, Madame Walker hired private tutors and read extensively. She continued to travel to promote her business for the rest of life. She died in 1919.

Walker's Legacy Madame Walker always was keenly interested in helping young black women become educated and independent. In addition to selling her products, many Walker agents opened their own beauty shops and became independent businesswomen. She used much of her wealth to support education for African American women. She established scholarships at several black women's schools and colleges. She also supported the National Association for the Advancement of Colored People (NAACP), homes for the aged, and various projects to promote black artists and writers.

Madame Walker left her company to her daughter. She directed in her will that the company always be headed by a woman. In the 1920s, A'Lelia Walker became well known in her own right as a patron of Harlem's talented black artists, writers, and musicians. Her support helped spur the Harlem Renaissance and the many intellectual and creative achievements of African Americans at this time. Madame Walker's granddaughter and then her great-granddaughter ran the Madame C. J. Walker Manufacturing Co. until it was sold in the mid-1980s.

A. P. Giannini

The son of immigrants started a bank for "the little fellow" that grew into the largest bank in America.

Having come from an immigrant family himself, Amadeo Giannini set out to help other immigrant families.

Immigrants' Son

In 19th-century America, banks were very conservative institutions. For example, bankers made it a practice to lend money only to wealthy or middle-class people. It was very difficult for poor people, especially recent immigrants, to borrow money to buy farmland or homes or to start businesses. In 1904, Amadeo P. Giannini, whose parents had come to America from Italy, started a small bank to lend money to other Italian immigrants. He built the bank into the largest in the United States.

Giannini was born in 1870 in San Jose, California. He was the son of Luigi and Virginia Giannini. His father, a farmer and a hotelkeeper, was murdered by a laborer when Amadeo was only seven. His mother married a man named Lorenzo Scatena. In 1882, Scatena took the family to San Francisco, where he opened a wholesale business buying and selling produce (fresh fruits and vegetables). When Giannini was 13, he quit school and went to work for his stepfather. He was a hard worker and so good at his job that Scatena made him a partner six years later.

A Bank in America

At the age of 31, Giannini sold his half of the thriving produce business to his employees for $100,000 and "retired." He intended to support himself and his family with income from real estate investments he had made. Little did he know that he was soon to become a banker.

A New Bank Less than a year after Giannini's retirement, his father-in-law, Joseph Cuneo, died. He left Giannini with a large estate to manage. Cuneo had owned shares in the Columbus Savings and Loan Society. A savings and loan bank specializes in housing loans. One of the duties Giannini had inherited was membership on the bank's board of directors. He became concerned about the bank's refusal to lend money to Italian immigrants or to members of other immigrant groups. When Columbus Savings refused to liberalize its lending policy, Giannini resigned from the board and opened a rival bank directly across the street. He called it the Bank of Italy. The $150,000 start-up money included investments from his stepfather and nine friends.

From the start, Giannini intended his bank to be for "the little fellow." He routinely loaned money to farmers, merchants, and laborers—most of them Italian immigrants. Small fruit and vegetable growers borrowed money from the Bank of Italy to help plant and harvest their crops. Giannini even loaned small sums—up to $300—to workers on their signatures alone.

Two Quakes Two major events won Giannini a widespread reputation for dependability and resourcefulness. In 1906, when a disastrous earthquake struck San Francisco, Giannini raced to his bank building in a vegetable wagon. Arriving just ahead

of the fire that was sweeping through the downtown area, Giannini piled the bank's gold and other assets into the wagon, covered them with vegetables, and drove off through roaming mobs of looters. Giannini set up a temporary bank in a shed on the waterfront. His bank was the only one that was able to open for business. And he quickly set about lending money to San Franciscans, enabling them to rebuild their homes and businesses.

Then, a year later, a brief panic rocked the nation's financial markets. Giannini had foreseen the unstable position that banks were in and had stockpiled a large amount of gold. In the aftermath of the crash, he was able to give his depositors hard cash, while other banks issued IOUs (paper promises to pay).

A Banking Empire As Giannini's banking business grew, he bought banks in other towns and turned them into branches of the Bank of Italy. His was the first branch banking system in the United States. Giannini's dream was to build a bank so large that it would have branches all across the country. By the end of the 1920s, he had branches throughout California. In 1928, he established the Transamerica Corporation to act as a management company for all of his far-flung businesses, which by now included insurance companies and businesses in other industries as well as banking. The following year, he combined the Bank of Italy with other banks he had acquired under the name Bank of America.

◄ This is a busy Bank of America branch in San Francisco as it looked in 1943.

One of the first bank credit cards in America was offered by Giannini's Bank of America.

America's Largest Bank

By the time Giannini retired as active head in 1945, the Bank of America had become the largest bank in the United States. It had more than $6 billion in money and property, 3 million customers, and nearly 500 branches. It financed most of Hollywood's major motion picture studios.

But as the bank had grown in size, it had also aroused criticism. During the Great Depression of the 1930s, some people cautioned that it was too powerful—that the big bank had forgotten "the little fellow." For example, the bank was criticized for foreclosing, or taking the property of thousands of bankrupt farmers. Foreclosed land was often bought up by larger landowners and agribusinesses (big commercial farming operations) that had the money to spend. In the late 1940s, the U.S.

government began investigating concerns that the Bank of America and Transamerica had violated federal antitrust laws (laws against monopolies). In the early 1950s, the government forced the companies to limit their holdings.

Giannini died in 1949 at the age of 79, while the antitrust suit was still pending. Before he died, he had used his wealth to create several charities, including the Giannini Agricultural Foundation to benefit the University of California.

The Bank Today The Bank of America continued to grow and change after Giannini's death. In the 1950s, it introduced one of the first bank credit cards in America—the BankAmericard (now called VISA). Today the bank started by A. P. Giannini is one of the largest in the world.

Alfred Fuller

The original
"Fuller Brush Man,"
he created a new model
for door-to-door selling.

A Twisted-Wire Brush

From America's earliest days, peddlers have wandered the streets and roads of America selling goods and services to homemakers and farm families. In colonial times, traders took to the back roads on foot or by horse and wagon. Later, thousands of European immigrants made their start in America peddling fruits, vegetables, useful items for sewing, and all manner of goods from house to house. They carried heavy packs or maneuvered pushcarts through crowded city streets. Alfred Fuller helped bring door-to-door peddling into the 20th century.

Born on a farm in Nova Scotia, Canada, in 1885, Fuller was the 11th of 12 children. He left home at the age of 18 in 1903 to seek his fortune in Boston. He worked at a variety of jobs until 1905, when he was hired as a salesman for a brush and mop company. After a year on the job, Fuller had learned much about brushes and had saved $375. He used some of that money to set up a workshop in the basement of his sister's house. There he made twisted-wire brushes and founded a company.

As a brush and mop salesman, Alfred Fuller gained the experience he needed to start his own business.

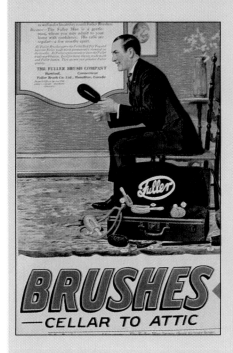

Fuller Brush salesmen were known for being courteous and helpful. One Fuller salesman changed a customer's tire.

Knocking on Doors

Fuller made his brushes at night and sold them door-to-door during the day. Encouraged by his early success, Fuller decided to move his company to Hartford, Connecticut, a city he had visited on sales trips. He set up shop in a rented shed. Fuller first called his company the Capitol Brush Company, but he learned that another company already had that name. So he changed the name of his enterprise to the Fuller Brush Company.

A National Company By 1910, Fuller was so successful that he employed 25 salesmen and 6 factory workers. He was selling Fuller brushes throughout New England, New York, and Pennsylvania. In 1911, Fuller placed a small advertisement for salesmen in a national magazine. Within a few months, he had recruited more than 100 salesmen. Soon they were peddling Fuller brushes across the United States.

The Secret of His Success Fuller always claimed that the secret to his success as a door-to-door salesman was that he always tried to be unfailingly polite and helpful. He also had a carefully researched sales pitch. As he recounted in his autobiography: "I would knock on the door and say, 'Good morning, madam, if there is anything wrong in your house that a good brush could fix, perhaps I can help you.'"

Fuller said that he sold his first brush to a housewife who used it to clean a radiator. "After that I studied a housewife's needs and we made a brush for every need," he said. The company's products eventually included more than 700 kinds of brushes. The "calling card" of the Fuller Brush Company was a free vegetable brush, called "the handy," that salesmen gave to each customer. Millions of "handies" were handed out over the years.

By 1947, the company's sales had reached $30 million. Fuller's brush salesmen were independent contractors, each of whom had a territory that covered about 2,000 homes.

They purchased the products from the company at wholesale prices and kept whatever profit they made by selling them at a retail price. Women salespersons—called "Fullerettes"—were added in 1948 to help market a line of cleaning supplies and cosmetics. By the 1970s, more than 25,000 salespeople worked for the Fuller Brush Company in the United States, Canada, and Mexico.

Fuller's Philosophy It took a special breed of person to sell door-to-door. Life for a Fuller Brush seller was a constant stream of rejections and slammed doors. The turnover among salespersons was high. Typically, only two of every seven people hired lasted for any length of time.

Fuller was aware of the difficulties of the job and sought to build morale with company songs, pep talks, bonuses, commissions, and the free use of a company park and clubhouse. He was a very optimistic and energetic man who liked to tell his workers that *"American* ends with 'I can' and *dough* [money] begins with 'do.'"

Still Selling Brushes

After Fuller Alfred Fuller served as president of the Fuller Brush Company until 1943 and chairman of the board until 1968. Two of his sons ran the company until it was sold to Consolidated Foods in 1968. At the time of Fuller's death in 1973, the company was showing an annual income of $130 million.

Today, an estimated 12,000 to 18,000 distributors still sell Fuller Brush products at markets, fairs, and house parties. The products are also sold through telemarketing and direct mail and directly to businesses. Some salespeople still go door-to-door, but that is not common any more. Many of the distributors are women. The company still specializes in brushes, brooms, and mops. It also sells cleaning supplies, including a line of "environmentally friendly" products.

An American Institution Fuller Brush men and women became a familiar sight throughout the country over the years. They had a reputation for being persistent but polite and helpful, just as Fuller himself was. Like other traveling sellers, the Fuller Brush Man became the subject of many jokes. At least two movies—*The Fuller Brush Man* starring Red Skelton and *The Fuller Brush Girl* starring Lucille Ball—poked fun at the occupation. Alfred Fuller did not mind the jokes and parodies—he considered them free advertising. They helped make Fuller Brush into a familiar American institution.

A BRUSH FOR EVERY CHORE

Refrigerator coil brush   Wet mop   Grout brush   Lambswool duster   Window brush

Alfred Fuller prided himself on developing a brush to fit every cleaning need. Here are a few of them.

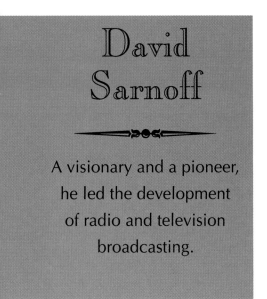

David Sarnoff

A visionary and a pioneer, he led the development of radio and television broadcasting.

David Sarnoff *(left)* is shown with Guglielmo Marconi, the inventor of radio, at the RCA transmitting center in Riverhead, New York.

Riding the Airwaves

When David Sarnoff took a job as a wireless operator in 1906, radio technology was very young. Radios were used solely to transmit messages in Morse code across distances in place of telegraph wires. Experiments with transmitting human speech by wireless were just taking place. No one had yet imagined that, within 20 years, radios would be in many American homes. Television had not even been invented yet. Sarnoff was a bright young man who thought of new uses for radio and then television when both inventions were still in their infancy. His career would earn him the title of "the father of American television."

Coming to America Sarnoff, a Russian Jew, was born in 1891 in a small town near Minsk. When he was nine, his family immigrated to New York. Two days after they arrived, young Sarnoff went to work to help support his family. He sold newspapers, worked for a butcher, and sang in a synagogue choir. When Sarnoff was 15, his father died. He quit school to take a job as a messenger

boy for a telegraph company. This was the beginning of a lifelong career in broadcasting.

Learning the Business With his first paycheck, David Sarnoff bought a telegraph instrument and taught himself Morse code. Six months later, he went to work for the Marconi Wireless Telegraph Company—first as an office boy and later as a telegraph operator. The Marconi company posted Sarnoff at telegraph stations on Nantucket Island, Massachusetts; at Coney Island, New York; and aboard various ships. In 1912, department store owner John Wanamaker hired Sarnoff to operate a powerful radio station he had installed on the roof of his New York store. It was there that Sarnoff gained momentary fame on April 14, 1912. He was the first to receive news of the sinking of the great ocean liner *Titanic*. Sarnoff stayed at his post for 72 hours sending and receiving news of the disaster.

A Set in Every Household

The Radio Music Box By 1915, Sarnoff was working as a manager for the Marconi company. That year, he proposed an idea to the company's general manager for what he called a "radio music box." He imagined a radio set—built by the Marconi company—in every American household. The radio would receive music and other broadcasts. Sarnoff's bosses did not find his idea practical at the time. But Sarnoff continued to rise to positions of ever greater responsibility in the company.

In 1919, the Radio Corporation of America (RCA) bought the Marconi company. Sarnoff became general manager of RCA in 1921. Meanwhile, a Westinghouse engineer had begun regular radio broadcasts in Pittsburgh on KDKA, the nation's first commercial radio station. Knowing that the time for his idea had come, Sarnoff again proposed his radio music box—this time to the president of RCA. He also arranged to give a demonstration of the radio by broadcasting a boxing match between heavyweight champion Jack Dempsey and challenger Georges Carpentier. The broadcast was heard by some 200,000 people—mostly amateur radio operators and hobbyists with homemade radios. The president of RCA was impressed by the broadcast, and the company soon began manufacturing radio receivers. And David Sarnoff received a promotion—to vice president.

The new radio sets were so popular that the company sold more than $80 million worth within three years. In 1926, Sarnoff helped RCA establish the National Broadcasting Company (NBC) to provide nationwide programming and sell national advertising for the new medium. By 1930, he had become president of RCA.

The Miracle of Television In the late 1920s, Sarnoff had hired Vladimir Zworykin, one of the inventors of television. He urged Zworykin to perfect his device for broadcasting moving pictures through the airwaves. In 1939, Sarnoff unveiled television to the public at the New York World's Fair. Thousands of fairgoers peered into a box and saw a flickering image of Sarnoff himself announcing, "Now at last, we add sight to sound." Two years later, in 1941, RCA established the first commercial television station, WNBT-TV, in New York City.

Further development of television was delayed when the United States entered World War II at the end of 1941. Sarnoff, a reserve officer in the signal corps, was called to active duty in 1944. He served as General Dwight Eisenhower's communications consultant for the remainder of the war, rising to the rank of brigadier (one star) general.

Year	Number of U.S. Households with TVs (Thousands)	Number of TV Stations
1946	8	30
1950	3,875	104
1955	30,700	469
1960	45,750	626
1965	52,700	681
1970	59,000	881
1975	69,000	953
1980	76,000	1,011
1985	85,000	1,182
1990	92,000	1,442

THE GROWTH OF TELEVISION OWNERSHIP AND STATIONS 1946–1990

Source: *Statistical Abstracts*

In the early years, television was more a curiosity than a success. But as it gradually caught on, the number of families owning television sets and the number of television stations increased by great leaps.

This photo, taken in 1953, shows Sarnoff holding the magnetic tape that is used to record television pictures.

The Peacock

For the rest of his life, Sarnoff's employees always called him "the general" or "General Sarnoff." In 1947, David Sarnoff retired as president of RCA and became chairman of the company's board of directors.

During the late 1940s and early 1950s, television became a huge commercial success. Television stations spread across the country, and millions of people bought TV receivers. Many popular radio programs were adapted for television, and many new types of programming were created.

Color Added In the early years of television, sets received only black-and-white pictures. Sarnoff kept pushing his company to develop color broadcasting. By 1961, when the public began demanding color sets, RCA was far ahead of its competitors. Its television network, NBC, adopted a logo of a peacock with multicolored feathers. This told viewers that they could see its programs in color if they purchased a color set.

Star Player Over several decades as president and board chairman, Sarnoff ruled his broadcasting empire from an office on the 53rd floor of "Radio City," the RCA office complex in New York City. He retired from the chairmanship of RCA in 1970 and died in 1971, having played a starring role in developing radio and television into the major industries they are today.

Roy Herbert Thomson

He started with a small Canadian radio station and built a worldwide media empire.

A Barber's Son

Roy Herbert Thomson was born in Toronto, Canada, in 1894, the son of a barber and a hotel maid. When he was 14, Thomson quit school and went to work as a clerk for $5 a week. Over the next several years, he tried his hand at a number of occupations before fighting in World War I. After the war, Thomson failed at a number of business ventures, including farming and selling automobile parts. Then in 1928, he made a fresh start in Ottawa selling radio sets. That was in the very early days of radio.

In those days, few people in Canada's sparsely settled northern regions bought radios. Broadcasting stations were too far away, and the sets picked up only static. Thomson realized that he could increase the sales of his radios if he started a broadcasting station of his own. In 1931, during the depths of the Great Depression, he borrowed $500, purchased a transmitter, and headed north. He launched radio station CFCH in North Bay, Ontario. That tiny station was the beginning of what would become an enormous media empire.

A Canadian's Empire

Prospering in Canada In 1933, Thomson started a second radio station even farther north, in Timmins, Ontario. The following year, he purchased a small weekly paper that was published in the same building. Over the next 20 years, he purchased six more radio stations throughout northern Canada and incorporated them into the Northern Broadcasting Network. He also bought five more newspapers, mostly in Ontario. Then in 1951, he entered the budding television business by establishing a station in Canada.

Thomson's business strategy was to use the profits from the stations and newspapers he already owned and to borrow heavily to buy new businesses. Whenever he met another publisher or station owner, he would ask, "Do you want to sell?"

Invading Britain Thomson's wife of 36 years, Edna, died in 1951. The following year, he began campaigning for election to the Canadian Parliament but was eventually defeated. Thomson was already very wealthy, but those two losses left him restless. He began to look around for new interests.

In 1953, Thomson extended his newspaper holdings to Great Britain by purchasing a daily newspaper in Edinburgh, Scotland. For Thomson, the descendant of Scottish immigrants, buying *The Scotsman* was like coming home. He moved to Edinburgh and turned over his Canadian properties to his son, Kenneth. "I look on myself as a Scot," he declared. "I am going to live in Scotland and I am going to die in Scotland." The following year, Thomson established a television station in Scotland. Earning huge profits from the station alone, he once referred to it as "a license to print money."

Off to London In 1959, the Kemsley Newspaper Group sold its chain of newspapers to Thomson for £31.5 million. This gave him control of 4 Sunday papers, 11 dailies, and 8

In the 1970s, many newspapers converted to computerized typesetting. Lord Thomson is shown here trying out the new system.

After receiving the title of baron in 1964, Lord Thomson (*center*) became a member of the House of Lords, Britain's upper legislative chamber.

First Baron of Fleet

Queen Elizabeth II awarded Thomson a title in 1964—first Baron Thomson of Fleet—for his service to British journalism. Although he greatly enjoyed his wealth and his title, friends say that Thomson was unassuming, friendly, and easy to talk to. He often ate breakfast at a truck stop, and he welcomed all kinds of visitors to his office, from important officials to ordinary people.

At the time of his death in 1976, Thomson owned 148 newspapers, including about 50 small dailies and weeklies in the United States. He also owned 138 magazines, several book-publishing companies, and numerous television and radio stations.

Those who knew Roy Herbert Thomson have described him as a shrewd businessman and risk taker. When he was asked the secret of his success, he replied, "no leisure, no pleasure, just work."

weeklies throughout Great Britain. The jewel in the crown of the Kemsley group was the *Sunday Times.* Published in London, it had a circulation of almost one million readers. Thomson restructured the *Sunday Times.* He bought new presses and added a new full-color magazine section, the first in Great Britain.

In 1967, he also bought one of the world's most respected newspapers, *The Times* of London. (This paper had no connection with the *Sunday Times*). Because of rising paper and labor costs, *The Times* was losing money badly. Thomson supported the newspaper with his own personal fortune for more than 15 years because, he once said, "It's unthinkable that it should die. *The Times* of London is Britain to many people."

A Hands-off Policy Thomson was primarily a financier whose main interest was in making money from his investments. "I am in business to make money, and I buy more newspapers to make more money to buy more newspapers." Although he tended to be conservative politically, he established a hands-off policy toward his newspapers. He left editorial

direction in the hands of the editors. "My papers are community papers," he once said. "It would be foolish for me to try to tell an editor in . . . Moose Jaw what his community needs; he lives there, knows the people he serves and what they should have in the way of editorial interpretation."

Thomson owned publishing companies, broadcast media, and a 20 percent interest in an offshore oil venture.

Milestones in Lord Thomson's Life

1894	Born on June 5
1931	Started a radio station in North Bay, Ontario
1933	Opened another radio station, in Timmins, Ontario
1934	Bought the *Timmins Press,* a weekly newspaper serving a gold-mining town; turned newspaper into a daily
1944	Owned eight radio stations and five newspapers; moved to Toronto and continued acquiring newspapers, including several in the United States
1953	Bought *The Scotsman* and moved to Edinburgh to oversee its operation
1957	Started Scottish Television Limited
1959	Bought Kelmsley Newspaper Group
1963	Became a British citizen
1964	Received title of Baron Thomson of Fleet
1967	Bought *The Times* of London
1972	Entered a North Sea venture with Occidental and Getty Oil
1976	Died on August 4

Walt Disney

His cartoon characters, movies, and theme parks have enchanted millions of children of all ages.

Walt Disney draws Mickey Mouse, his most famous character and the one for which he received an Oscar in 1932.

A New Medium

At the dawn of the 20th century, motion pictures were a new invention. They had no sound, and they were shot only in black and white. Animated cartoons were also new. The first animated cartoons were one- or two-minute advertisements shown between feature films. They were also silent and filmed in black and white.

It was during these early days that Walt Disney learned the art of animation. He was one of the first people to recognize the potential of animation as an art form and as a source of amusement. He understood that animated films could be enormously entertaining.

Disney's World Walt Disney was born in Chicago, Illinois, in 1901 and was raised in Missouri. When he was very young, he realized that he wanted to be an artist. When Disney was still in elementary school, he began taking lessons at a local art school on Saturday mornings. The Disney family moved back to Chicago when Walt was 16. He went to high school there and took art courses at night. In 1918, during World War I, he dropped out of school to become an ambulance driver.

The Disney Studios

Becoming a Cartoonist After the war, Disney took a job as an apprentice cartoonist with a Kansas City advertising company. There he first learned how to make animated cartoons. Intrigued by the new art form, Disney set up his own small animation studio in his father's garage. He made a series of humorous short cartoons he called Laugh-O-Grams. However, he found it difficult to persuade local theater owners to show them. In 1923, Disney headed for Hollywood, the moviemaking capital of America. There he joined his brother Roy, who was already working in the motion picture industry.

The two brothers combined their savings and set up a new cartoon studio. That early studio, which also began in a garage, was the beginning of Walt Disney Productions. Roy was the studio's business manager, and Walt was its creative head. By 1927, the studio employed a large group of artists. Walt Disney rarely did any drawing himself by then, instead directing the artists to depict his ideas.

The Birth of Mickey Walt Disney's earliest Hollywood productions were "Alice in Cartoonland" and "Oswald the Rabbit," but his most famous and most enduring creation was Mickey Mouse. The idea for Mickey Mouse came to Disney while he was on a train trip from New York to California. Before the trip ended, Disney had already planned a whole new cartoon series for a mouse character. At first, he was going to call him Mortimer, but he settled on Mickey at the suggestion of his wife.

Mickey Mouse first appeared in the cartoon *Steamboat Willie* in 1928. The first cartoon to include a sound track, it was a huge hit—and so was Mickey. Over the next few years, other now familiar Disney characters made their first appearances in Mickey Mouse cartoons, including Minnie Mouse, Donald Duck, Pluto, and Goofy.

By the 1930s, the Disney Studios staff had grown to more than 100 employees, who were creating the popular Mickey cartoons and other cartoon "shorts." But Disney was

DISNEY ANIMATED AND FEATURE FILMS			
Animated Films		**Feature Films**	
Steamboat Willie	(1928)	Treasure Island	(1950)
Snow White and the		The Living Desert	(1953)
Seven Dwarfs	(1937)	The Vanishing Prairie	(1954)
Fantasia	(1940)	20,000 Leagues Under the Sea	(1954)
Pinocchio	(1940)	Davy Crockett	(1955)
Dumbo	(1941)	Swiss Family Robinson	(1960)
Bambi	(1942)	The Absent-Minded Professor	(1961)
Cinderella	(1950)	Mary Poppins	(1964)
Peter Pan	(1953)	The Love Bug	(1969)
Sleeping Beauty	(1959)	Pete's Dragon	(1977)
101 Dalmatians	(1961)	Splash	(1984)
The Jungle Book	(1967)	Who Framed Roger Rabbit?	(1988)
The Little Mermaid	(1989)	Dead Poets' Society	(1989)
Beauty and the Beast	(1991)	Honey, I Shrunk the Kids	(1989)
Aladdin	(1992)	Dick Tracy	(1990)
The Lion King	(1994)		

In the 1950s, Disney began producing films with live actors. And by the 1990s, the Disney company was distributing films made by others.

planning a bigger project—a movie-length cartoon in full color and with music. Given the time-consuming nature of animation, the project would be costly and risky. In 1937, Disney released *Snow White and the Seven Dwarfs,* the first feature-length cartoon ever made. *Snow White* took Disney's animators three years to complete and cost more than $1.6 million, a large sum in those days. The investment paid off in many ways, for the movie was a great technical achievement and a smash success.

Snow White was the first of many Disney animated films based on fairy tales and popular children's stories. Throughout the 1940s and 1950s, the Disney Studios produced many other feature-length cartoons, including *Pinocchio, Fantasia, Dumbo, Bambi, Cinderella, Alice in Wonderland, Peter Pan,* and *Sleeping Beauty.*

New Worlds to Build

Movies and Television In the 1940s, Disney began to produce animal documentaries. In the 1950s, the studio began making motion pictures with live actors. *Treasure Island,* based on the Robert Louis Stevenson novel, was the company's first live-action film. It was soon followed by *20,000 Leagues Under the Sea, Old Yeller,* and *Mary Poppins,* an experimental combination of live action and cartoons.

Disney also expanded into the new medium of television in the early 1950s with *The Mickey Mouse Club,* an afternoon children's show, and later with *Walt Disney Presents,* an evening program that showed cartoons, films, and documentaries. Walt Disney himself hosted the program and became a familiar face to millions of Americans. Film and television successes, combined with earnings from the many products featuring Disney characters, made him a very wealthy man.

Building a Dream Walt Disney was always looking for new projects to undertake. One of his most ambitious ideas was to build a theme park based on his characters. The park, Disneyland, cost $50 million to build. But from the moment it opened its gates in 1955 in Anaheim, California, it was one of the world's most popular tourist attractions. Almost as soon as Disneyland was finished, Walt Disney started to plan another kind of park—which he called the Experimental Prototype Community of Tomorrow (EPCOT)—that would reflect his vision of the future.

Tomorrowland Disney died in 1966 before EPCOT became a reality. A version was later incorporated into Disney World in Orlando, Florida. Disney theme parks have also been built in Japan and France. The Disney Corporation is currently planning an American history theme park in Virginia.

Walt Disney's company, now a huge entertainment corporation, continues to produce live-action films, animated cartoons, and theme parks to delight future generations.

Characters from Disney movies march down Main Street in the Magic Kingdom in Orlando, Florida.

Ray Kroc

As the founder of McDonald's Corporation, he revolutionized the fast-food industry—and the way Americans eat.

Fast Food

Before the abundance of fast-food restaurants that we know today, families dining out went to a restaurant or a diner. They sat down, ordered their food, and waited while it was cooked. Going out to eat was relatively expensive and time-consuming. Because of that, families dined out much less often than families do today. But Ray Kroc and a small take-out food business in California changed all that.

Making Milk Shakes Ray Kroc was born and raised in the suburbs of Chicago, Illinois. He quit school at 16. Lying about his age, he trained to become an ambulance driver in World War I. (He served in the same company as Walt Disney.) When the war was over, Kroc worked at various jobs—sometimes two or three at a time. For 16 years, Kroc sold paper cups. Then he began a new venture. In 1937, he became the sole distributor for a milk shake machine. This machine led Kroc to McDonald's.

By the mid-1970s, Ray Kroc was the chairman of the board of McDonald's and the owner of the San Diego Padres.

McDonald's outsells its nearest competitor by more than three to one.

Building the Golden Arches

Take-out Food Kroc started his own small company to sell the machines and built a very successful business. In 1954, he became curious about two brothers in San Bernardino, California, who sold so many milk shakes that they had bought eight of his machines—more than any other customer. The brothers, Mac and Dick McDonald, had hit on a formula for high-volume food sales. They ran a take-out food stand and had sold franchises for seven others. (A franchise is the right to sell the products or services of a particular business.) The brothers limited their menu to hamburgers, french fries, and milk shakes and provided paper sacks so that customers could carry their food away.

A Chain of Restaurants Drive-in restaurants like those of the McDonald brothers were something of a fad in California during the 1950s. However, Ray Kroc had the idea of expanding the McDonald business into

SALES FIGURES FOR LEADING U.S. RESTAURANT CHAINS, 1992	
Restaurant	Sales (millions of dollars)
McDonald's	$21,885
Kentucky Fried Chicken	6,700
Burger King	6,400
Pizza Hut	5,700
Wendy's	3,613
Hardee's	3,400
Taco Bell	3,300
Domino's Pizza	2,400
Little Caesars	2,050
Subway	1,750
Arby's	1,517
Jack In The Box	1,040

Source: *Restaurants and Institutions*

a nationwide chain of drive-ins that were all alike. He thought that if he could arrange with the brothers to sell franchises, he could also greatly increase the sales of his milk shake machines. The McDonald brothers agreed. Kroc became their agent to sell franchises across the United States. Each new restaurant would use the McDonald name and the brothers' system of food preparation and service.

Kroc opened his first McDonald's restaurant on April 15, 1955, in Des Plaines, Illinois, a suburb of Chicago. It had no tables or seats, just a counter where people could walk up and place an order. The take-out restaurant was an immediate success, and the McDonald's chain took off. By 1960, Kroc had sold about 220 franchises. The following year, he bought out the McDonald brothers completely. He paid $2.7 million for the right to use their name and their service system. He continued to build thousands of new McDonald's restaurants all over America—and soon all over the world.

In 1977, a Ronald McDonald House for terminally ill children opened in Chicago.

The Same Food Everywhere One of the secrets of Kroc's success was his insistence on providing uniform quality and preparation of each food item. That way customers always know what to expect when they walk into a McDonald's—under the well-known golden arches. A Mc-Donald's hamburger in Duluth, Minnesota, tastes exactly the same as one in Spartanburg, South Carolina.

Kroc's successful formula also included offering a small number of menu items that could easily be mass-produced. Cooking equipment was designed to make food preparation fast and efficient. The limited menu also meant that customers became familiar with McDonald's food. As new items were added, they were given catchy names, often using the company's prefix "Mc."

As with any good idea, McDonald's restaurants soon generated much competition. Although several other fast-food chains also have grown very large, McDonald's remains the largest in the world.

An American Institution

Giving Back Ray Kroc's restaurants made him a multibillionaire. Kroc, who died in 1984, enjoyed his wealth. Among other things, he used it to purchase the San Diego Padres baseball team. He also believed in giving something back to the community for its support and patronage. He established the Kroc Foundation, which gave money for medical research. Kroc also founded Ronald McDonald Houses. These are guest houses for families of seriously ill children who are undergoing long hospital treatments.

Hamburger Flipping Kroc's impact on America goes far beyond expanding the fast-food industry. Because burger flipping is a low-paying, entry-level job, fast-food restaurants provide the first employment opportunities for millions of American teenagers. McDonald's also provides work opportunities for senior citizens and people with mental and physical disabilities.

McDonald's has faced criticism over the years and reacted to changes. Environmentalists protested the chain's heavy use of foam packaging, which adds to pollution. In the late 1980s, the company switched to paper wrappings and began promoting recycling.

Nutritional concerns about McDonald's foods led to other changes. The chain began providing nutritional information in the late 1980s. It also added salads and other low-fat foods to its menu.

McDonald's restaurants have become one of the most visible symbols of American enterprise around the world. Today, there are nearly 14,000 McDonald's restaurants throughout the United States and in 72 countries, including Russia, Morocco, Saudi Arabia, Israel, and China. McDonald's has also established a permanent place for itself in American culture. Kroc's first McDonald's Restaurant in Des Plaines is now a museum, preserving an era when hamburgers cost 15 cents.

Hundreds of Russians lined up outside Moscow's first McDonald's restaurant, which opened in 1990. The restaurant is equipped to make and sell about 15,000 meals a day.

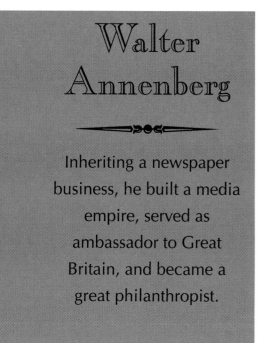

Walter Annenberg

Inheriting a newspaper business, he built a media empire, served as ambassador to Great Britain, and became a great philanthropist.

Top Magazines by Gross Revenue and Circulation

Magazine	Combined Revenue[1]	Paid Circulation
TV Guide[2]	$595.0	15,604,267
Reader's Digest	327.4	16,264,547
People	296.6	3,208,667
Time	254.2	4,094,935
Sports Illustrated	215.4	3,220,016
National Geographic[3]	211.4	10,189,703
Consumer Reports	98.3	4,849,173
Good Housekeeping	96.5	5,152,521
Life	66.5	1,844,482
Money	65.5	1,915,053
Rolling Stone	42.6	1,229,280
Seventeen[2]	31.6	1,772,362
Car & Driver	22.4	959,395

[1]Subscriptions plus newsstand revenues (millions of dollars)
[2]Annenberg publications
[3]Sold by subscription only

Source: *Advertising Age*

The Family Patriarch

Walter Annenberg's story begins with his father, Moses, a German Jew who immigrated to the United States with his family in 1885. The Annenbergs settled in Chicago, where 12-year-old Moses went to work to help support his family. In 1900, Moses took a job in the circulation department of William Randolph Hearst's new Chicago newspaper, the *Tribune*. Moses Annenberg rose rapidly in the Hearst organization. He used his earnings to buy newsstands, real estate, and two newspapers of his own, the *Daily Racing Form* and the *Morning Telegraph*. These papers catered to horse race bettors.

By the time Walter Annenberg was born in 1908, Moses Annenberg had become quite wealthy. Moses adored his only son. He sent him to private schools and later took him into the family business, Triangle Publications. In 1940, things changed. Moses Annenberg was charged with failure to pay his income tax. Walter, then a vice president of the company, was also charged. To protect his son, Moses pleaded guilty and spent two years in prison.

After Moses Annenberg *(left)* died, Walter Annenberg took charge of the family business.

Annenberg's Inheritance

Moses Annenberg died soon after his release from prison. Walter inherited Triangle Publications, which then consisted of the two racing newspapers and the Philadelphia *Inquirer,* a large morning newspaper. Annenberg also inherited his father's debt—$4 million owed to the federal government in back taxes. No one expected much from the young Annenberg. He was a shy man who was handicapped by a stutter and deafness in one ear. People knew him as the son who stood quietly in his father's shadow. But Walter Annenberg was determined. He set out not only to run Triangle and expand it, but to pay the money owed to clear his father's name.

New Ideas for Changing Times

Walter Annenberg first made himself the publisher and editor of the *Inquirer.* He then purchased a second Philadelphia newspaper, the *Daily*

◀ Two Annenberg publications—*TV Guide* and *Seventeen*—are compared with other popular magazines.

News, and bought several magazines and radio stations.

In 1944, Annenberg noticed that there were no publications for teenage girls despite their growing buying power. He started *Seventeen* magazine, which was a huge success. Its first issue alone sold 400,000 copies. A few years later, Annenberg established WFIL-TV in Philadelphia, only the 13th television station in the United States. He later bought several more TV stations throughout the country.

Filling a Need Owning television stations made Annenberg aware of the need for a publication that listed TV programs. A few such magazines already existed in some major cities. Annenberg's idea was to create a national magazine with regional editions that combined local program listings with articles of interest to all TV viewers.

When Annenberg launched *TV Guide* in 1953, it was a huge and risky investment that counted on the rapidly rising popularity of the new medium—television. The risk paid off quickly, and *TV Guide* soon became Triangle's biggest moneymaker.

Annenberg remained chairman of Triangle until 1988, when he sold the company to Australian media giant Rupert Murdoch for $3.2 billion. He had previously sold the Philadelphia *Inquirer* and *Daily News* to publisher John S. Knight for $55 million in 1969.

Serving and Giving

Seeking Acceptance Walter Annenberg had achieved enormous wealth, but he still pursued two lifelong goals—to restore his family's reputation and to be accepted by his peers in society. For many years, he kept a plaque on his desk that read "Cause my works on earth to reflect honor on my father's memory." One way he sought to clear his father's reputation was to establish a charitable organization in his name, the M. L. Annenberg Foundation. In 1962, he endowed a graduate school, the Annenberg School of Communications at the University of Pennsylvania, also dedicated to his father.

With his family history and background, however, Walter Annenberg found it more difficult to win acceptance in high society. In 1969, President Richard Nixon appointed him ambassador to Great Britain, the most important ambassadorship a President can bestow. Annenberg's appointment generated a great deal of criticism, some of which drew on his past and some on his conservative political views. Many people doubted that he would be up to the task. But Annenberg surprised his critics by carrying out his duties competently. He even forged a friendship with the British royal family. In fact, he was the only U.S. ambassador to be knighted by Queen Elizabeth.

Giving It Away After serving as ambassador, Annenberg retired to Southern California with his wife. Their desert estate contains many fine artworks and antiques that the Annenbergs collected over the years. He now devotes himself to sharing his multibillion-dollar fortune to help others. In 1991, the Annenbergs gave their collection of about 50 Impressionist paintings to the Metropolitan

President Clinton looks on as Walter Annenberg announces his most generous gift—$500 million to aid public education.

Museum of Art in New York City. Valued at more than $1 billion, the collection now gives pleasure to hundreds of museum visitors every day.

Annenberg's favorite recipients are schools, colleges, and cultural institutions. He has made several major gifts in these areas in recent years, including

- $50 million to the United Negro College Fund.
- $100 million to the Peddie School, a private school in New Jersey that he attended as a teenager.
- $120 million to the University of Southern California to establish a school of communications.
- $150 million to the Corporation for Public Broadcasting.

Annenberg's most spectacular gift was a $500 million grant in 1993 to improve public education.

In later years, Walter Annenberg placed another plaque on his desk. This one, a quote from former British prime minister Winston Churchill, read "Look not for reward from others but hope that you have done your best."

Sam Walton

His chain of discount stores transformed the small towns of the South and the Midwest.

According to *Fortune* magazine, Sam Walton's vacations usually included trips to competing stores.

Life Before Wal-Mart

For generations, people had done much of their shopping for clothing and household goods in downtown department stores and variety (five-and-dime) stores. After the Great Depression and World War II, Americans enjoyed an era of prosperity. Many people bought homes in the suburbs and new automobiles. The downtown stores gave way to shopping centers and malls built on the outskirts of cities and towns. People could do their shopping at modern, spacious stores where parking was plentiful and free.

Nationwide retail chains—such as J. C. Penney and Sears, Roebuck and Co.—concentrated their big new department stores in large towns and densely populated suburbs. Chain officials passed over small towns, believing that these places could not support large stores.

In the small towns of the South and the Midwest, people continued to shop at small stores on "Main Street." Sam Walton, who grew up in just such a small town, brought his own chain of large retail stores to these overlooked small towns and changed them forever.

From a Small Town Samuel Moore Walton was born in Oklahoma in 1918. When he was a small child, his family moved back to their native state of Missouri. The Waltons settled in Shelbina, a town of about 2,000 people. When Walton was a sophomore in high school, the family moved again to a larger town, Columbia—the home of the University of Missouri.

Sam Walton began working when he was a freshman in high school, doing odd jobs and delivering the local newspaper. He also worked part-time in a local variety store. But he had no plans then to become a retailer. After high school, he worked his way through the University of Missouri, graduating in 1940. Walton's first job after college was as a management trainee at a J. C. Penney store in Des Moines, Iowa. There he learned two important principles of retailing:

- Put customer satisfaction first.
- Motivate employees to provide good service by giving them a stake in the success of the business.

Ben Franklins After World War II, Walton purchased a Ben Franklin variety store franchise in Newport, Arkansas. He might have remained a small-town shopkeeper for the rest of his life if it had not been for an unexpected event. In 1950, he lost his lease and had to move his franchise and his family to a new town—Bentonville, Arkansas. Walton lived there for the rest of his life.

Throughout the 1950s, Walton and his younger brother, James, opened 15 Ben Franklin stores in cities and towns throughout Missouri and Arkansas. Tired of spending so much time traveling from store to store by car, Sam Walton bought a small private plane and learned to fly.

Wal-Mart Takes Off

One of the secrets of Walton's success was that he kept up with the latest trends and new ideas in retailing. When other stores began to change to self-service so that customers did not have to wait for clerks to serve them, Walton followed suit. When large discount stores caught on with the public, Walton launched his own chain of discount stores. He called the chain Wal-Mart.

Sam Walton noticed that other discount chains had opened their stores in larger towns and cities. He was determined to concentrate on smaller towns. The first Wal-Mart Discount City opened in Rogers, Arkansas, in 1962. A second in nearby Harrison soon followed. Walton began flying around the region scouting locations for new Wal-Marts on the outskirts of small towns. Over the next 30 years, he built a chain of stores that now consists of more than 1,700 stores and about 425,000 employees.

Walton lured customers by offering "everyday low prices," a wide variety of goods, and extended shopping

The Wal-Mart concept of an "everyday low price" brings a steady flow of customers.

hours. He also created elaborate promotions to bring people into his stores. For people in many small towns, the local Wal-Mart became the place to go on Saturday afternoons.

In the 1980s, Walton branched out into wholesale warehouse clubs, where people could buy merchandise in bulk for about 10 percent over the wholesale price (the cost to the store). By 1991, Walton had opened 200 of these stores, called Sam's Wholesale Clubs.

Walton's Legacy

One day in the early 1980s, Walton was surprised to discover that his chain of retail stores had made him the richest man in America. At the time of his death in 1992, his personal fortune totaled more than $20 billion. Despite his great wealth, he always remained a small-town boy. He lived in a three-bedroom house, drove a pickup truck, and had his hair cut at the local barbershop.

Although Walton loved small towns and their people, he did much to change the nature of the towns his stores served. In many towns served by a Wal-Mart, "Main Street" merchants—including long-established, family-owned stores— have been driven out of business. The merchants contend that they cannot compete with Wal-Mart's large variety of products and discount prices. In recent years, some small towns have begun to oppose the opening of new Wal-Mart stores.

Walton was aware of the changes his stores have caused. He wrote in his autobiography that he believed that Wal-Mart has done more good than harm to the dying small towns across America—by giving people a better place to shop. Indeed, by 1992, shoppers from these towns had helped Wal-Mart grow into one of the nation's largest retailers.

LARGEST U.S. RETAILING COMPANIES		
Company	No. of Employees	No. Stores
Wal-Mart	425,000	1,720
Sears	403,000	1,824
Kmart	356,000	2,249
J. C. Penney	192,000	2,510
Kroger	190,000	2,203
Dayton Hudson	170,000	770

Sources: *Fortune, Hoover's Handbook of American Business*

Today, Wal-Mart is one of the largest retail chains in the United States.

Phil Knight

The founder of Nike, Inc., he created a worldwide demand for specialized athletic shoes.

The Coach's Running Shoes

Philip "Buck" Knight grew up in a suburb of Portland, Oregon. He was the son of a newspaper publisher. In the 1950s, Knight was a mile runner on the University of Oregon track team under the man who was America's top college track coach, Bill Bowerman. At that time, only a few companies sold sneakers and athletic shoes in the United States. Athletes had few choices of styles or features when buying shoes for their sports.

During his years at Oregon, Bowerman experimented with the running shoes he had. He took them apart and put them back together with different kinds of soles and uppers to make them lighter. He believed that shaving an ounce or two off the weight of the shoes helped his athletes run faster.

A few years later, Knight was studying business at Stanford University. Remembering Bowerman's homemade shoes, he wrote a paper on marketing running shoes for a class on small businesses. In the paper, he argued that high-quality running shoes could be made inexpensively using labor in Asia. The shoes could then be sold in the United States for less than other shoes. That paper contained the idea that would make Knight a billionaire.

Phil Knight completed his studies at Stanford in 1962. After graduation, he decided to travel for a while before settling down to an office job.

Phil Knight entered a partnership with his former college track coach, Bill Bowerman. Knight would handle the daily operation of the business; Bowerman would provide design ideas, test the shoes, and recommend them to other coaches he knew.

Winged Victory

While visiting Japan, Knight learned that the Japanese were making imitations of Adidas track shoes under the brand name Tiger. Adidas is a German shoe company, which, along with Puma, another German company, dominated the American market for athletic shoes in the 1960s.

Tigers in the Basement Knight visited the manufacturer of Tiger shoes. He pretended to be an importer for a shoe company. He made up the name of the company on the spot—the Blue Ribbon Sports Company. When Knight returned home, he sent two pairs of Tigers to his old coach, Bowerman. Bowerman immediately agreed to be Knight's silent partner in the shoe-importing business.

Knight began to sell Tigers from the basement laundry room of his parents' house in Oregon for $6.95 a pair. To gain acceptance of his shoes, he sent samples to high school and college track teams. He also sold his shoes out of the back of a station wagon at track meets around the state.

Knight's business grew gradually. In 1965, he hired a salesman and opened the first Blue Ribbon Sports retail store in Santa Monica, California. Stores in Eugene, Oregon, and in Boston soon followed. Over the next few years, Knight opened five more retail stores.

The Birth of Nike As the Blue Ribbon Sports Company grew, it experienced frequent legal problems with its Japanese manufacturer and with a rival distributor of Tiger shoes. In 1971, Knight decided to launch a new company to produce its own line of shoes. He named the new company Nike after the Greek winged goddess of victory. The company adopted a

Sales of Nike shoes and clothing more than tripled in ten years.

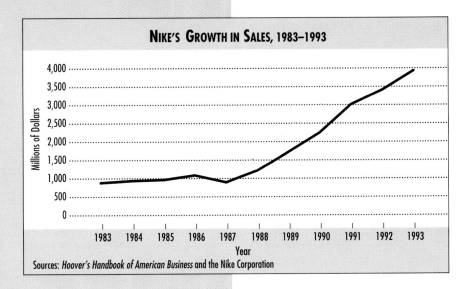

NIKE'S GROWTH IN SALES, 1983–1993

Sources: *Hoover's Handbook of American Business* and the Nike Corporation

logo that looked like a stylized wing. The logo, which is still used today, came to be called the "Swoosh."

A New Sole In 1972, Bowerman, who had continued experimenting with running shoe designs for the company, developed a new kind of sole. Called the waffle sole, it provided greater speed and traction for long-distance runners. His timing coincided perfectly with a growing interest in fitness and jogging. Throughout the 1970s, as jogging became a popular sport, the sales of running shoes skyrocketed. Nike's waffle-soled running shoes were a big hit. Soon they were being imitated by all Nike's competitors.

As the demand for sports and fitness equipment grew, Nike began

marketing specially designed shoes for many kinds of sports—basketball, aerobics, tennis, football, and baseball. Knight, who runs and plays tennis, personally tests Nike's new shoe lines.

The Superstars A favorite Knight strategy in the company's early years was to pay as many athletes as possible to wear Nike gear. In the mid-1980s, that strategy changed. Nike decided to take a chance on one potential superstar athlete to represent the company—basketball player Michael Jordan. It was a brilliant choice. For years, Nike had tried to market a shoe with an air pocket in the sole, but its efforts had met with limited success. By 1985, Jordan had become a superstar, and Nike made a fortune selling the air-soled basketball shoes called Air Jordans. Nike then recruited another celebrity athlete—football and baseball star Bo Jackson—to help sell another line of air soles, Nike Airs.

As the superstar endorser of Nike gear, Michael Jordan "soars" above a busy Barcelona street during the 1992 Summer Olympic Games.

Knight and Nike Today

The athletic shoe industry has changed a great deal since Knight first went into business—partly as a result of his marketing ideas. Nike's shoes had helped stimulate the fitness trend in the United States. Along the way, athletic shoes had become more than tools for playing sports—they had become status symbols, especially among young people. Often commanding high prices, athletic shoes were no longer the inexpensive imports Knight began selling.

In 1983, Knight resigned as president of Nike. He currently serves as chairman of the board and is still the driving force behind the company. By 1993, Nike had reached $3.9 billion in sales. It commanded about one-third of the athletic-shoe market worldwide. Throughout its history, however, the company has faced stiff competition.

Philip Knight's personal wealth is estimated at $1.4 billion. In the athletic shoe industry, he is known as a fierce competitor and as a corporate leader who inspires great loyalty from his employees. To the public, he is most visible in his support (personally and through the company) of athletes and athletics everywhere.

Ted Turner

With his superstations and all-news network, he transformed television and TV news.

Ted Turner has been described as a mixture of fierce pride and nonstop speechmaking. He is shown here outside the CNN office in Atlanta, Georgia.

A Rocky Start

Ted Turner was born in Cincinnati, Ohio, in 1938. When he was nine years old, his father, Edward Turner, bought a billboard company in Savannah, Georgia, and moved his family there. Edward Turner raised his only son sternly, occasionally beating him. But Edward, who became a millionaire in the outdoor advertising business, also showered his son with gifts and sent him to expensive private schools. Edward Turner's dream was that his son would one day take over the billboard company.

When Ted was still in elementary school, he began working for his father during the summer, and he continued to do so through college. While at Brown University in Providence, Rhode Island, Turner was suspended for rowdiness and was eventually expelled for breaking dormitory rules. He joined the Coast

Guard and served six months. Then, in 1960, Turner joined his father's company as general manager.

Two years later, Edward Turner bought a large billboard company in Atlanta, Georgia, but the purchase strained the company's finances. The elder Turner signed an agreement to sell the Atlanta company and then committed suicide, leaving the ailing business to his son.

Superstations to Networks

Ted Turner was only 24 when his father died, but he soon proved to be an able businessman. His first step was to cancel the agreement to sell the Atlanta business. He quickly succeeded in turning the struggling company around. Soon Turner had set his sights on other media. In 1970, he purchased an independent television station in Atlanta and a second station in Charlotte, North Carolina. These two stations were the beginning of the Turner broadcasting empire.

Going National Successful broadcasters typically expanded by buying or starting new stations around the country. But Ted Turner had different plans, and these plans depended on two things—cable television and satellites. When Turner entered the broadcasting business, cable TV was a small industry that mainly served areas with poor reception. The federal government limited the access of broadcasters to cable systems. In 1975, at the urging of Turner and others, the government lifted these restrictions. That same year, a new satellite for communications was

Broadcasting news around the clock makes the CNN newsroom a perpetually busy place.

launched into orbit. Turner purchased the right to beam a television signal off the satellite to cable systems around the country.

In 1976, Atlanta station WTBS (named for the Turner Broadcasting System) began broadcasting to America's cable households. It was the first nationwide independent station, or "superstation." Turner's goal was to broadcast around the clock. He purchased two sports teams—the Atlanta Braves (baseball) and the Atlanta Hawks (basketball)—and broadcast their games. He also bought thousands of old movies, cartoons, and television reruns to fill more airtime. In 1979, Turner added news programs, special events, and children's shows, finally filling 24 hours of airtime.

A News Leader In 1980, Turner launched an all-news cable television station. Called the Cable News Network, or CNN, it was the first round-the-clock news network. It had a staff of 300 people working in a converted Atlanta country club. Many media experts thought that CNN would fail. After all, who would want to watch the news 24 hours a day? CNN not only succeeded, it revolutionized television news. It enabled people to watch worldwide events, such as the Persian Gulf War and the collapse of the Soviet Union, as they were happening.

Many world leaders watch CNN because it provides up-to-the-minute coverage. In some cases, hostile world leaders have used CNN to communicate with one another. During the Gulf War, for example, President George Bush sent a message to Iraqi officials through CNN reporters. The changes triggered by CNN were not without cost. World leaders now find themselves with much less time to react to crises, and war correspondents are more restricted in what they can report because of fears that they may broadcast information to the enemy.

Today CNN has a staff of 1,700 people in 28 bureaus (news offices) throughout the world. It is seen in over 150 countries. In addition to CNN, Turner started a second all-news channel, Headline News, and a general channel, Turner Network Television (TNT). This broadcasting conglomerate has made Turner an enormously wealthy man. His personal fortune is more than $2 billion.

Prince of the Global Village

Many Interests In his business, Turner has followed where technology has led, and he has rarely walked away from controversy. As a young man, he had a reputation for being hot-tempered. He still is widely known for being very outspoken. In fact, he has been nicknamed "the mouth of the South." In 1991, Turner married actress Jane Fonda, who is also famous for her outspokenness.

Turner strongly supports environmentalism, peace, and social justice. He is known for backing programs that explore these issues. In recent years, he has offended Native Americans by refusing to change the name of the Atlanta baseball team—the Braves. Nevertheless, in 1993, his network produced and broadcast a series of sensitive TV movies about Native American leaders. Turner has also been widely criticized for allowing many of the classic black-and-white movies he owns to be "colorized" by computer.

Man of the Year In 1992, *Time* magazine named Turner its Man of the Year, calling him the "Prince of the Global Village." His broadcast system has helped the world seem a smaller place. Global information and communications may someday make it a friendlier place.

Millions of viewers, including many world leaders, watched CNN as the Persian Gulf War unfolded in 1992.

Anita Roddick

She made low-key marketing, consumer education, and social activism the foundation of a new kind of retail business.

The Beauty Business

Cosmetic companies have typically sold their products through expensive advertising campaigns, extraordinary claims about their products, and aggressive selling. They often hire young, beautiful models to suggest that using these products will make customers look young and beautiful. Cosmetics companies may charge high prices for small quantities of perfumes, skin creams, and shampoos. They commonly make extravagant promises that their creams and lotions will erase wrinkles, change a person's looks, and ensure lasting love and happiness.

When Anita Roddick opened her first Body Shop in Brighton, England, in 1976, she sold hair and skin products in a different way. She used information and enthusiasm—but no advertising.

Anita Perella was born in 1942, the daughter of café owners in a small seaside town in southern England, and an unlikely candidate to turn the retail world on its ear. As a young woman, she was intent on becoming an actress. Before working on that goal, however, she took a trip around the world. The journey changed her life.

Making It Happen

After traveling throughout Europe, the South Pacific, and Africa, Anita Perella returned to England. She met and married Gordon Roddick, another "free spirit" whose lifelong dream was to ride a horse from Argentina to New York. In the spring of 1976, Gordon Roddick went to South America to fulfill his dream. To earn a living for herself and their two children, Anita decided to open a small shop. Starting with a $6,400 loan and little business experience, she stocked a line of about 20 natural skin- and hair-care products. These were products she had learned about from the peoples of various countries she had visited during her travels.

A New Kind of Business Roddick knew little about managing a business. She simply invented the rules as she went along. She had no money for advertising, so she did not advertise. She had only a few kinds of products to sell, so she offered them in different quantities. She could not afford new containers, so she began refilling old plastic containers for repeat customers. Because she did not want her employees pressuring customers, she trained them to simply be available to answer questions about the products. This combination of simplicity and service generated great loyalty and enthusiasm among her customers. Word of her store soon spread around town. In less than a year, Roddick's business had grown so large that she opened a second store. As her two Body Shop stores became more widely known, people began asking to buy franchises—the right to use the Body Shop name and sell its products. Soon Body Shop franchises began appearing throughout Europe and in North America.

Anita Roddick stands in front of one of her now famous Body Shop stores. The first opened in Brighton, England, in 1976.

Roddick has slogans painted on her delivery trucks to show her support for many social and environmental causes.

Roddick has continued to travel to faraway corners of the world several times a year searching for new natural products to add to her line. She requires that each product be safe to use and friendly to the environment. None of her products are tested on animals, which is a common practice in the cosmetics industry. But each is carefully researched. Complete information about each product's ingredients and its uses is available in pamphlets, flyers, and videos throughout the stores.

A Bent for Activism An important element of Roddick's personal philosophy is her belief that the Body Shop should give something of value back to the community and the world. She has adopted all kinds of social causes—such as saving the whales, recycling, and preserving the rain forests. While most big businesses avoid these kinds of controversial issues, Roddick is often seen at protest marches and demonstrations. Her delivery trucks carry messages about social concerns, and her stores

are collection points for donations to various causes.

Roddick admits that the free publicity generated by her activism helps advertise her stores. But she feels that it also helps to effect change and to educate her customers and employees.

A New Kind of Management Roddick believes that business should be fun, honest, and accountable to employees as well as customers. She feels that employees should enjoy their jobs and share in the company's success. She runs a company training program for employees and franchise owners that stresses learning the nature and uses of the Body Shop's products, not selling techniques. Although the Body Shops have made her very wealthy, Roddick says that she would find focusing a business only on profits "deeply boring."

In less than two decades, Anita Roddick created a new kind of cosmetics company and expanded it worldwide.

An Ongoing Concern

Roddick now has stores in over 40 countries. The shops stock hundreds of items and earn profits of more than $15 million a year. As managing director of the company, she is in charge of developing and marketing products. When she is not traveling to find new products, she supervises the manufacturing of the company's products and oversees the employee newsletter. Her husband, Gordon, oversees the financial and administrative aspects of the business.

The Body Shop's success and its unique marketing formula have inspired several imitators. These stores also offer natural, environmentally safe cosmetics and embrace social activism. Nevertheless, the Body Shop remains well ahead of these competitors. Roddick has shown that a company can gain loyal customers and succeed by simply providing product information rather than high-powered advertising and high-pressure selling.

The Body Shop Milestones	
1976	The first Body Shop opens in Brighton, England.
1978	The Body Shop expands out of England into Belgium.
1984	The company begins selling stock to the public, causing the value of the company to soar.
1985	Anita Roddick is named Britain's Businesswoman of the Year.
1987	The Confederation of British Industry names the Body Shop Company of the Year.
1988	The first shop is opened in the United States in New York City.
	Anita Roddick is awarded the Order of the British Empire by Queen Elizabeth.
1989	Anita Roddick is named Britain's Retailer of the Year.
1991	After 15 years in business, company sales total more than $238 million.

Ben Cohen and Jerry Greenfield

They founded an ice-cream company and now use the profits to support environmental and social causes.

Friends since junior high school, Ben Cohen (left) and Jerry Greenfield share many interests, including community involvement and ice cream.

Old Friends

Bennett Cohen and Jerry Greenfield first met in junior high school in Merrick, Long Island, in the early 1960s. They went through high school together, then separated to attend different colleges. Cohen studied art—jewelry making and pottery. Greenfield prepared in college for medical school, but he was not admitted to any. The two friends held various jobs during the early 1970s. They shared an apartment in New York City while Cohen worked as a hospital clerk and taxi driver and Greenfield worked as a laboratory technician.

They went their separate ways for two years and then moved in together once again, this time in Saratoga Springs, New York. Cohen and Greenfield had always talked about going into a small business together, and in 1977, they decided to do it. At first, they considered making and selling bagels, but the equipment was too expensive. Then they considered ice cream.

Starting a Company

Cohen and Greenfield had had some experience with ice cream. Cohen had driven an ice-cream van during his high school and college years, and Greenfield had scooped ice cream in college. But they had no experience making ice cream to sell, so they took a $5 correspondence course in ice-cream making from Pennsylvania State University. Pooling their resources—$4,000 each—and borrowing another $4,000 from a bank, they opened the first Ben & Jerry's ice-cream parlor in 1978. It was in a converted gas station in Burlington, Vermont.

Flavor of the Week Cohen and Greenfield's store was a success right from the start. They offered a rich, all-natural ice cream—at premium prices—that people lined up to buy. One secret to their early success was the unusual flavors they concocted. They sent away to food suppliers for flavor samples, then combined whatever samples arrived each day. One day they might offer Honey Apple

Raisin Oreo and the next Lemon Peppermint Carob Chip. Eventually, they hit on the idea of mashing up their favorite cookies and candy bars and mixing them with ice cream. Thus Chocolate Fudge Brownie and Heath Bar Crunch were created.

Another reason for Cohen and Greenfield's early success was their involvement in the local community. They sponsored free concerts and film festivals and distributed free ice cream at charity events.

A Fast-Growing Company The two entrepreneurs began packing their ice cream in large containers and selling it to restaurants throughout Vermont. Then they started selling pint containers in local grocery stores. The success of these ventures was so rapid that Ben & Jerry's ice cream was soon being sold in stores all across the United States. By 1990, Cohen and Greenfield

- had built a production plant.
- had started 82 ice-cream-parlor franchises.
- employed a staff of 350.

Social Activism

Since those early days in Burlington, the two men have been serious supporters of peace, environmentalism, anti-hunger crusades, education, and children's rights. They established the Ben & Jerry's Foundation, which distributes 7.5 percent of the company's pretax profits to charitable causes. For example, a portion of the profits from their Rainforest Crunch ice cream supports efforts to save the Amazon rain forest. Similarly, revenue from their Peace Pop ice-cream bars goes to various peace and social-justice organizations.

Cohen and Greenfield's philosophy that businesses have a responsibility to the community also affects how the company is run. Ben & Jerry's buys some of its ingredients to support particular groups—for example, brownies made by homeless people and Maine blueberries picked by Native Americans. The company also strives to be environmentally correct in its operations. For example, it gives ice-cream by-products to pig farmers to mix into their feed, rather than dumping the waste into local water supplies.

The company conducts an annual "social performance" assessment to see how well it is meeting its ideals and to evaluate the effectiveness of its various social programs. The direction of each year's major campaigns is partly determined by the issues employees are most concerned about.

Activist Employees Cohen and Greenfield believe that their employees should be involved in community programs and social causes. Employees earn "points" for volunteer work. These points count toward raises and promotions. The company also sponsors trips for employees to educate them about social issues. On one such trip, employees lived among the Cree Indians of Canada for several weeks. The Crees' land is threatened by a major project to produce hydroelectricity.

Too Much Commitment? Cohen and Greenfield do have their critics. Despite their progressive views, the two company owners have strongly discouraged unionization of their workers. Some employees and former

Workers on the production line are shown inspecting the solid ingredients—such as cherries—that are added to the ice cream.

employees also feel that the company pressures them too much to support its founders' liberal social causes. Some company executives have also criticized a policy introduced by Cohen that no executive could make more than five times the salary of the lowest paid worker. They noted that the policy affected all but Cohen and Greenfield, who have made millions from company stock.

Despite these criticisms, the company continues to flourish. In recent years, the two founders have spent less time in the day-to-day operation of the company and more time on the foundation and on their individual interests.

Visitors are invited to tour the Ben & Jerry's ice-cream plant in Waterbury, Vermont.

Steven Jobs

Working in a garage,
he helped invent
the personal computer,
making computer
technology accessible
to everyone.

Apple's first sale was to a local computer dealer who ordered 25 of them. This is what the first Apple computer looked like.

Big Machines and Big Ideas

In the early days of the information age—in the 1950s and the 1960s—computers were bulky, room-sized machines used primarily by the government, universities, and big businesses. Computer technicians and programmers needed extensive training to be able to use these complicated machines. To most people, computers were mysterious technological marvels. Relatively few people used them or understood them.

Steven Jobs was an orphan who was adopted as an infant by Paul and Clara Jobs in 1955. He became interested in computers as a high school student in Los Altos, California. His interest and his ability landed him a summer job at an office of the Hewlett-Packard computer company in nearby Palo Alto. There he became acquainted with a Hewlett-Packard employee named Stephen Wozniak, an engineering genius who liked to tinker with new inventions. Neither of them realized at the time that their meeting would change the world. Together they would make computers accessible to ordinary people.

A Revolutionary Computer

After high school, Jobs went to college, but he soon dropped out. In 1974, he took a job with Atari Inc., a company that made electronic games. Later that year, Jobs began attending meetings of a group of computer hobbyists called the Homebrew Computer Club. The club leader was Stephen Wozniak.

Wozniak just liked to play with computers, but Jobs began thinking about building and selling computers to other hobbyists. He persuaded Wozniak to join him, and the two of them designed the first personal computer in Jobs's bedroom.

The First Apple In 1976, Jobs showed a prototype, or model, of their first computer to a local retailer, who ordered 25 of the machines. Jobs sold his car and Wozniak sold his prized Hewlett-Packard scientific calculator. The two partners went into business with their combined resources—$1,300. They set up a production line in the Jobs family's garage and hired Jobs's sister to help them assemble the computer circuit boards.

The new company needed a name. Jobs came up with the name "Apple" and created a logo showing an apple with one bite missing. This was a pun on the word "byte," which is a unit of computer information. Within a year, Apple Computer had sold 600 of its first design, which was called the Apple I. The selling price was $666, and the buyers were mainly computer hobbyists.

The first Apple assembly line was in the Jobs family's garage in Cupertino, California. This one is in nearby Silicon Valley, a region of Northern California known for computer production.

Jobs donated thousands of Apple computers to school districts. Because many students learned on these computers, their parents bought Apple computers for home use. In this way, Jobs gained a large share of the personal computer market.

Jobs paid independent programmers to write programs for the Apple II. Soon there were several thousand programs, such as VisiCalc and AppleWorks, that users could purchase. Jobs also gave away thousands of Apple IIs to school districts around the country so that teachers could teach children how to use computers.

A Growing Company Apple kept growing larger and larger, adding more employees and executives. Within six years, it was recording annual sales of more than $500 million. By 1981, competitors, like the giant IBM, also began to market personal computers. Over the next several years, Apple developed more innovative machines. In 1984, it introduced the Macintosh, which became very popular. The Macintosh pioneered an especially easy-to-use method in which a mouse (like the directional device on a video game) is used to choose commands.

After Apple

Apple made Steven Jobs and Stephen Wozniak multimillionaires. In 1985, Jobs left Apple Computer after clashing with John Scully, who had been hired to run the company. Jobs started a new company to market a new computer. He called it "NeXT." Although NeXT computers were well received by university and business users, they were too expensive for home use. They never found a large market.

Only a few years ago, the idea of owning and operating a computer was unthinkable to most people. Today, millions of people in the United States and all over the world own computers and are comfortable using them. Computers are everywhere—in stores, schools, libraries, and offices. Many people even carry portable computers so that they can work at home or while traveling. Almost overnight, the computer industry went from making only big machines to serve corporations and government to creating ever smaller, more powerful, and easier-to-use machines and software for every home and office. The vision of Steven Jobs helped make computers part of everyday life for millions of people.

Friendly Computers Soon Jobs and Wozniak had to move Apple from the garage to an office and a factory. Wozniak supervised production, and Jobs handled marketing. In 1977, the company launched the Apple II, the first computer for beginners and general users. It consisted of a beige plastic box with a keyboard and sold for about $1,400.

This early personal computer had two features that made it user-friendly for untrained buyers. It was the first small computer to contain an on-board read-only memory (ROM)—a permanent program that tells the machine how to load the software programs people would use. The second feature was a built-in connecting device that enabled users to hook up the computer to a monitor or a television receiver easily. Users could then see what they were doing when working at the computer.

Getting the Programs Jobs realized that, for the new machines to become popular, they had to be useful as well as easy to use. They needed software programs so that users could perform different tasks—writing, editing, accounting, record keeping, and games.

In the late 1980s, Jobs formed a new company to market a new computer. He is shown here demonstrating the NeXT computer.

Glossary

agribusiness: A large, commercial farming operation; a combination of the terms "agriculture" and "business."

antitrust laws: Laws designed to restrict or break up the power of large business combinations in order to prevent monopolies.

apprentice: A person learning a trade or craft, usually under the supervision of a skilled worker.

Bessemer process: A method of making steel from pig iron by burning out the impurities with forced hot air.

cable system: A television system in which distant station signals are picked up by a single, large, elevated antenna and transmitted by cable to the homes of paying subscribers.

carob: The sweet pod of a Mediterranean evergreen tree; used as a flavoring, especially as a substitute for chocolate.

communications satellite: A satellite, launched into orbit around the earth, that is used to enhance worldwide communication. Broadcasters beam their signals to the satellite, where they are then reflected back to the earth at a different location.

competition: Rivalry between two or more businesses striving for the same customers or markets. Each business seeks to offer the most favorable prices and terms.

conservative: Tending to be traditional in outlook and generally opposed to change.

consumer goods: Products, such as food and clothing, that satisfy human needs and wants.

crude oil: Petroleum; a flammable liquid obtained from drilling oil wells into the earth. A major industrial raw material, it is refined into gasoline, kerosene, and other fuel oils.

discount chain: A group of stores belonging to the same company that sell products to consumers at reduced prices.

dry goods: Fabric, clothing, and sewing items.

entrepreneur: A person who organizes, manages, and assumes the risk of a business venture with the expectation of gaining a profit.

environmentalism: Concern with the quality of the environment, especially the effects of air pollution.

fast-food restaurant: A restaurant where food is prepared and served quickly.

financier: A person who deals with money and investments on a large scale.

foreclose: To take possession of a mortgaged property because the conditions of the mortgage, such as monthly payments, have not been met.

franchise: Permission given to a dealer to sell the goods or services of a particular company.

incorporate: To combine with something else; to form or become a corporation.

Industrial Revolution: The change from an agricultural to an industrial society that occurred in the 18th and 19th centuries as a result of many new inventions.

internal-combustion engine: An engine that runs on a fuel mixture that is ignited and burned within the engine.

liberal: Tending to be unbound by traditional forms or beliefs; recognizing the need to adapt and change conditions.

Linotype machine: A typesetting machine that is operated by a keyboard and that sets each line of type in one piece.

marketing: The process of buying and selling in a market; the commercial functions involved in getting goods from the producer to the consumer.

monopoly: The exclusive ownership or control of a product or service that results in a lack of competition.

Morse code: A system that combines dots and dashes (or long and short sounds) to represent letters of the alphabet and numerals; used to transmit messages by telegraph.

peddler: A salesperson who travels around selling goods, especially from house to house.

personal computer: A microcomputer; a high-tech machine that processes and stores information for easy retrieval.

pomade: A perfumed ointment for the hair and the scalp.

refinery: A building with equipment used for removing impurities from metals, petroleum, sugar, and other substances.

retail: The sale of goods in small amounts to the actual user.

retail chain: A number of stores owned or managed by the same company that sell goods in small amounts directly to the consumer.

serge de Nîmes: A strong, durable fabric made in Nîmes, France, from which the word "denim" is derived.

sharecropper: A farmer who leases land in exchange for a portion of the harvest.

social activism: Forceful action taken by an individual or a group in the service of a cause.

stockpile: To reserve or hoard a supply of an essential commodity for use during a shortage.

trademark: A special logo, name, or design, protected by law, that identifies the manufacturer of a product.

trust: A combination of firms or corporations, established by a legal agreement and controlled by a board of trustees.

typesetting: The setting in place of type in preparation for printing on paper.

unionization: The act of organizing a labor union to help workers secure good wages, benefits, and working conditions from their employer.

waffle sole: A kind of sole, developed by Nike, Inc., that provides greater speed and traction for long-distance runners.

wholesale: The sale of goods in large quantities, especially to retail stores and other businesses that resell them to consumers.

wireless: Having no wires. Wireless communication includes radio and telegraph.

"yellow journalism": A term referring to journalism that is more concerned with entertainment and sensationalism than with factual, objective reporting.

Suggested Readings

Note: An asterisk (*) denotes a Young Adult title.

*Bowman, John. *Andrew Carnegie.* Silver Burdett Press, 1989.

*Bundles, A'Lelia. *Madame C. J. Walker.* Chelsea House, 1991.

*Canadeo, Anne. *Sam Walton: The Giant of Wal-Mart.* Garrett, 1992.

*Crisman, Ruth. *Hot Off the Press: Getting the News into Print.* Lerner, 1991.

*Fanning, Jim. *Walt Disney.* Chelsea House, 1994.

*Fleming, Thomas. *Behind the Headlines: The Story of American Newspapers.* Walker & Co., 1989.

*Franck, Irene M., and Brownstone, David M. *Communicators.* Facts on File, 1986.

Greenia, Mark W. *Computers and Computing: A Chronology of the People and Machines That Made Computer History.* Lexikon Services, 1990.

Hearst, William Randolph, Jr., and Casserly, Jack. *The Hearsts, Father and Son.* Roberts Rinehart, 1991.

Henderson, Amy. *Pioneers of American Broadcasting.* Smithsonian, 1988.

*Henry, Sondra, and Taitz, Emily. *Everyone Wears His Name: A Biography of Levi Strauss.* Dillon Press, 1990.

Inglis, Andrew. *Behind the Tube: History of Broadcasting.* Focal Press, 1990.

Lewis, Tom. *Empire of the Air: The Men Who Made Radio.* HarperCollins, 1993.

*Little, Jeffrey B. *Understanding a Company.* Chelsea House, 1988.

Love, John F. *McDonald's: Behind the Arches.* Bantam, 1986.

Nash, Gerald D. *A. P. Giannini and the Bank of America.* University of Oklahoma Press, 1992.

*Older, Jules. *Ben and Jerry . . . The Real Scoop!* Chapters Pub., 1988.

Pollard, Sidney, editor. *Wealth and Poverty: An Economic History of the Twentieth Century.* Oxford University Press, 1990.

Robinson, Judith. *Hearsts: An American Dynasty.* Avon Books, 1992.

*Rozakis, Laurie. *Steven Jobs.* Rourke, 1993.

*Schuker, Nancy. *John D. Rockefeller.* Silver Burdett Press, 1989.

*Stefoff, Rebecca. *Ted Turner: Television's Triumphant Tiger.* Garrett, 1992.

Stephens, Mitchell. *A History of the News: From Oral Culture to the Information Age.* Viking Penguin, 1988.

Strasser, J. B., and Becklund, Laurie. *Swoosh: The Unauthorized Story of Nike and the Men Who Played There.* Harcourt, 1993.

Trimble, Vance H. *Sam Walton: The Inside Story of America's Richest Man.* Dutton, 1990.

*Van Steenwyk, Elizabeth. *Levi Strauss, The Blue Jeans Man.* Walker & Co., 1988.

Walton, Sam, and Huey, John. *Made in America.* Doubleday, 1992.

Index